A Fine Brush on Ivory

A Fine Brush on Ivory

An Appreciation of Jane Austen

Richard Jenkyns

OXFORD

UNIVERSITY PRESS

OXFORD
UNIVERSITY PRESS

Great Clarendon Street, Oxford ox2 6DP

Oxford University Press is a department of the University of Oxford.
It furthers the University's objective of excellence in research, scholarship,
and education by publishing worldwide in

Oxford New York

Auckland Bangkok Buenos Aires Cape Town Chennai
Dar es Salaam Delhi Hong Kong Istanbul Karachi Kolkata
Kuala Lumpur Madrid Melbourne Mexico City Mumbai Nairobi
São Paulo Shanghai Taipei Tokyo Toronto

Oxford is a registered trade mark of Oxford University Press
in the UK and in certain other countries

Published in the United States
by Oxford University Press Inc., New York

British Library Cataloguing in Publication Data
Data available

Library of Congress Cataloging in Publication Data
Data applied for

ISBN 0–19–927661–7

1 3 5 7 9 10 8 6 4 2

Typeset by Regent Typesetting, London
Printed in Great Britain
on acid-free paper by
Biddles Ltd,
King's Lynn, Norfolk

To Isabel Jones
Great(×5)-niece of Jane Austen

Preface

As you cross the border from Sussex the sign reads, 'Hampshire—Jane Austen's county'. Only one other English county identifies itself by a literary son or daughter in this way, but then Warwickshire does have Shakespeare to boast about. Dickens too was Hampshire born, but even if he had not left in infancy, he might have some trouble in competing with Jane Austen now. For her star seems to go on and on rising; the recent spate of film adaptations may be over, but though they may have put her in the news, they were essentially the consequence, not the cause of her popularity. Nor has her accessibility and the favour of the common reader put off the highbrows: her reputation among academics and intellectuals today seems to be higher than ever. Meanwhile, her vast readership enables her to be described in superlatives. She has possibly given pleasure to more men in bed than any other woman in history, except perhaps Agatha Christie. As many men may have fancied themselves in love with Elizabeth Bennet as with Claudia Schiffer. *Pride and Prejudice* is likely to be the most re-read book in English. And more than with any English author bar Shakespeare, her admirers have wanted to know about her life, which was famously not very long and not very eventful: in 1997 three new biographies appeared at almost the same moment. 'Jane

Austen and . . .' books abound: there are studies of her in relation to food, music, theatre, the clergy—works which often illuminate quiet corners of social and cultural history. And since her œuvre is not large, every part of it has been closely scrutinized.

A writer may feel some embarrassment, therefore, at adding to the pile of books about her. My reason is essentially that I thought myself to have something to say. Anyway, the deed is done, and in Mr Darcy's words, 'farther apology would be absurd'. This essay does not have one single thesis to argue. Readers may recognize some broad themes: form, pace, and proportion, and their relationship to literary meaning; how character is represented; the nature and effect of comedy; and other things. In other words, I raise and discuss some general and theoretical questions. But the book would be equally well described as a discussion of some individual novels. It is not a study of Jane Austen's work as a whole. I have written mostly about three novels, *Pride and Prejudice*, *Mansfield Park*, and *Emma*; I have also said a certain amount about *Sense and Sensibility*, but rather little about *Northanger Abbey* or *Persuasion*, and almost nothing, as it happens, about the other completed work of her maturity, the novella *Lady Susan*. Her other extant writings comprise *Sanditon*, the draft of a novel on which she was working until she became too ill to continue, *The Watsons*, the fragment of an abandoned novel, the letters, the juvenilia, and a few miscellanea (verses, prayers, *jeux d'esprit*, etc.); all these things have been in my mind while writing, though they may be mentioned only cursorily, if at all. In this book, when I refer to 'the novels' or 'the canon' I shall mean the six completed books, excluding *Lady Susan*. By 'the heroines' I shall mean the seven women who are the novels' protagonists, *Sense and Sensibility* having two joint protagonists in Elinor and Marianne. 'The heroes', similarly, will be the men whom these women marry.

I would not have tried to read the modern literature on Jane Austen exhaustively, even if that were possible. I did briefly entertain the notion of trying to write this essay rapidly and without any recourse to secondary literature at all, other than the memory of what I had already read, in the hope that spontaneity and independence might compensate for other deficiencies, but soon abandoned it, for a number of reasons. In the event, I have read quite widely in modern criticism and scholarship, with profit, though without changing my views significantly. Readers familiar with recent debate may notice that I have sometimes indicated my grounds for dissenting from other scholars' views implicitly, and on occasion explicitly. My title derives, as many readers will recognise, from Jane Austen's notorious description of her work as 'the little bit (two Inches wide) of Ivory on which I work with so fine a Brush, as produces little effect after much labour'. The context of these words is flippant, however: they come from a letter to her nephew in which she plays with a fantasy about stealing some of his adolescent prose to use in a novel of her own. In Jane Austen's writing— in her titles, even— we should always be ready for irony.

R.J.

Acknowledgements

For many years I have talked from time to time about Jane Austen's novels, as about other books, with friends, without having the slightest idea that I would ever write anything about her, and I probably owe more to long forgotten conversations than I now realize. I am aware of having benefited from Jasper Griffin, Henry Jenkyns, Viola Jones, Bryan Magee, Ann Schofield, Voula Tsouna, and Nicolette Vincent, but this is a list which should probably be much longer. Thanks also to Carol Heaton and Will Francis at Greene and Heaton, to Jackie Pritchard for copy-editing, and at Oxford University Press to Lydia Davis, Coleen Hatrick, Philip Henderson, Andrew McNeillie, Elizabeth Prochaska, and Frances Whistler.

Contents

Beginnings

Let us begin with a famous beginning—the first sentences of *Pride and Prejudice*:

> It is a truth universally acknowledged, that a single man in possession of a good fortune must be in want of a wife.
> However little known the feeling or views of such a man may be on his first entering into a neighbourhood, this truth is so well fixed in the minds of the surrounding families, that he is considered as the rightful property of some one or other of their daughters.

This pair of aphorisms stands like the two pillars of a proscenium framing the stage. They are entirely generalized; they sit apart from the narration. Then abruptly the general gives way to the particular; the curtain rises, and we are plunged immediately, without so much as a word of explanation about the setting or the characters, into the first scene of a comic drama:

> 'My dear Mr. Bennet,' said his lady to him one day . . .

And the rest of the chapter, until the last paragraph, is pure dialogue, more like what we expect from a play than a conventional novel (Jane Austen is perhaps, after Dickens, the most theatrical of English novelists; she loved play-acting in her youth). The perky inflection of ' "Mr. Bennet," said his lady' deftly signals the genre: we learn at once from the tone, as clearly as from the first tune in a Rossini overture, that this is to be a comedy.

The playwright cannot, as the novelist can, explain his characters and their situation through narrative; everything must emerge through dialogue. Jane Austen jettisons the novelist's advantage, and takes up the playwright's technique instead. The leading lady will not appear until the second scene—that is, the second chapter: in this first chapter we hear first that the Bennets have five daughters; then Lizzy's name, with the first hints that she has rather different relationships with her father and mother, is slipped into the last third of the conversation, so that we suspect that she is to be the heroine of the story. Thus the central character's first entrance is anticipated but held back for the moment; that again is classic technique for the playwright ('Let us impart what we have seen tonight Unto young Hamlet'; 'I thought the king had more affected the Duke of Albany . . .'; the bloody sergeant's praise of 'bold Macbeth'; and so on). Finally, the first chapter is rounded off with a short paragraph summing up the characters of Mr and Mrs Bennet and the nature of their marriage:

> Mr. Bennet was so odd a mixture of quick parts, sarcastic humour, reserve, and caprice, that the experience of three and twenty years had been insufficient to make his wife understand his character. *Her* mind was less difficult to

develop. She was a woman of mean understanding, little information and uncertain temper. When she was discontented she fancied herself nervous. The business of her life was to get her daughters married; its solace was visiting and news.

Such character vignettes are not uncommon in fiction, but usually they come before the characters have been set in action and tell us what to think about them, like the hostess slipping us a few facts about the other guests as we arrive. We expect such character sketches to introduce, but here they summarize. Jane Austen's judgement of the Bennets seems beautifully unmanipulative because it crystallizes and clarifies what we suspect that we have already learnt from listening to them talking to each other (the dialogue itself is masterly, and ought properly to be analysed sentence by sentence). To adjust the theatrical metaphor a little, the ironically detached sentences of aphorism and summary at either end frame the chapter; everything in between is pure 'stage action', unmediated by authorial comment. Indeed, the author effaces herself to such an extent that most of the dialogue in this first chapter comes without any formal indication of the speaker: once the dialogue has been set in motion there are in fact some two dozen changes of speaker with only one 'replied his wife' and one 'replied he' to interrupt the marital conversation—since there is absolutely no 'scenery' it is rather like listening to a play on the radio. Simply as technique, this is remarkably bold, free, and original.[1]

She has learnt from the theatre; but there was another public space that she knew much better. She will have heard readings from the Psalms in church almost every week of her life: their rhythms, with verse answering to verse, or half-verse to half-verse, echoing, amplifying, or explaining, were bound to sink deep into her consciousness:

> The heavens declare the glory of God: and the firmament sheweth his handiwork.
> One day telleth another: and one night certifieth another.

Such are the rhythms that open *Pride and Prejudice*; let us hear that beginning again:

> It is a truth universally acknowledged, that a single man in possession of a good fortune must be in want of a wife.
> However little known the feeling or views of such a man may be on his first entering into a neighbourhood, this truth is so well fixed in the minds of the surrounding families, that he is considered as the rightful property of some one of other of their daughters.

The first of these sentences is almost always quoted on its own, but Jane Austen presents them as a pair, versicle and response.

I do not suppose a conscious influence but an instinctive sense of balance and rhythmic expansion, nurtured in a world where the words of the Bible were all around one, in the air, as it were. The modern reader, however, is likely to think in terms of another tone: the famous opening of *Pride and Prejudice*, not least because of its very familiarity, may strike us as an instance of the 'eighteenth-century' Miss Austen, neat, tart, epigrammatic in an orderly way, a purveyor of 'What oft was thought but ne'er so well expressed'. In fact, it is radically innovative.

One way of beginning a story is by what one might call mood setting, when physical description is combined with the evocation of an atmosphere that is as much moral as sensory. Such is Dickens's realization of a muddy, fogbound London at the start of *Bleak House*. That does not occur in Jane Austen, though there are moments in her later work— such as the use of symbolic landscape and the evocation of moral space in *Mansfield Park*—which open the possibility that it might not have been altogether beyond her power. A more straightforward method of beginning is the cinematic technique. This is Dickens again, opening *Our Mutual Friend*:

> In these times of ours, though concerning the exact year there is no need to be precise, a boat of dirty and disreputable appearance, with two figures in it, floated on the Thames, between Southwark Bridge which is of iron, and London Bridge which is of stone, as an autumn evening was closing in.
>
> The figures in this boat were those of a strong man with ragged grizzled hair and a sun-browned face, and a dark girl of nineteen or twenty, sufficiently like him to be recognisable as his daughter. The girl rowed, . . . [and so on, for many more sentences]

This is in the style of the cinema: we see a visual image, with moving figures, the significance of which we do not yet understand; we keep watching, and we piece together the sense of the scene. Dickens wants to bring out the reader's— one might say the spectator's—uncertainty: the two figures in the boat, he notes, 'obviously were doing something that they often did, and were seeking what they often sought'. This is a technique that Hardy liked (at the start of *Tess of the D'Urbervilles*, for instance), but we do not associate it with Jane Austen, in whom physical description is so sparing. Yet the manuscript of *Sanditon* begins thus:

A Gentleman & Lady travelling from Tunbridge towards that part of the Sussex Coast which lies between Hastings and E. Bourne, being induced by Business to quit the high road, & attempt a very rough Lane, were overturned in toiling up it's long ascent half rock, half sand.—The accident happened just beyond the only Gentleman's House near the Lane—...

The beginning of *Sanditon* as it stands is scarcely more than the rough summary of an idea: one can hardly even call it a draft (though as the manuscript proceeds Jane Austen starts to develop more detail). But it does look as though she meant to open neither with information nor dialogue but with pure scene—a coach, a lane, an upset—and only later to introduce the dramatis personae and explain their circumstances. This device is strikingly original for its date and again suggests in Jane Austen—what the world does not expect from her—a search for technical experiment.

In *Anna Karenina* Tolstoy, presumably unaware of the precedent, follows *Pride and Prejudice* in beginning with an aphorism: 'All happy families are alike, but every unhappy family is unhappy in its own way.' But after this opening flourish, he proceeds in the conventional way, with some economical scene-setting. The conventional method is well shown by an authoress even more precocious than Jane Austen, Daisy Ashford in *The Young Visiters*:

Mr Salteena was an elderly man of 42 and was fond of asking peaple to stay with him. He had quite a young girl staying with him of 17 named Ethel Monticue. Mr Salteena had dark short hair and mustache and wiskers which were very black and twisty. He was middle sized and he had very pale blue eyes. He had a pale brown suit on but on Sundays he had a black one and he had a topper every day as he thorght it more becoming. Ethel Monticue had fair hair done on the top and blue eyes. She had a blue velvit frock which had grown rarther short in the sleeves. She had a black straw hat and kid gloves.

One morning Mr Saltccna came down to brekfast . . . [etc.]

This is a 9-year-old, late-Victorian child's idea of how a story ought to begin, and it thus suggests what a reader might naturally expect. I do not quote it because I think it a bad beginning; on the contrary, it is very good. It sets the scene in general terms, but mingles with the generalities several telling little particulars. It then moves smoothly into a dialogue between a man and a woman—the pattern of *Pride and Prejudice,* except that *Pride and Prejudice* has the pattern the other way round.

The King of Hearts thought that you could have the verdict before most of the evidence (and his wife wanted the sentence before the verdict)—all part of Wonderland's topsysturvydom. But it is a common procedure in novels, especially at the beginning. If Daisy Ashford seems too remote from Jane Austen, here is something much closer, the first sentences of Maria Edgeworth's *Belinda* (1802):

Mrs Stanhope, a well-bred woman, accomplished in that branch of knowledge, which is called the art of rising in the world, had, with but a small fortune, contrived to live in the highest company. She prided herself upon having established half a dozen nieces most happily; that is to say, upon having married them to men of fortunes far superior to their own. One niece still remained unmarried—Belinda Portman, of whom she was determined to get rid with all convenient expedition. Belinda was handsome, graceful, sprightly and highly accomplished; . . . [etc.]

This writing is as accomplished as Belinda herself, quietly tart, both setting a tone and drawing the reader quickly into the story. Indeed, in tone and content the opening of *Emma* is quite close:

> Emma Woodhouse, handsome, clever, and rich, with a comfortable home and happy disposition, seemed to unite some of the best blessings of existence; and had lived nearly twenty-one years in the world with very little to distress or vex her.
>   She was the youngest of the two daughters of a most affectionate, indulgent father, ... [etc.]

This is even more accomplished, but as a beginning it is, compared with *Pride and Prejudice*, more conventional.

The trouble with a brilliantly original stroke is that it cannot easily be repeated, and no other novel of Jane Austen's will open as *Pride and Prejudice* had done (on the first page of *Persuasion* she will bring off another brilliant but quite different coup). The pattern that she establishes here— first evidence directly presented, then the verdict—will return later in the book. Thus, a paragraph on Mr Collins's character, explaining his natural deficiencies and how the circumstances of his upbringing have made them worse, opens the fifteenth chapter; but it is held back until we have been able to see and hear him for ourselves, in the two chapters before. A page on Mr Bennet and his relationship to his favourite daughter, with an account of how he came to marry a woman so unsuitable to him and the effect of the marriage on his style of life, comes when more than half of the book is already gone (in volume ii, chapter 19). This is a subtle technique, which appeals to the emotion of recognition. Ah yes, we say, that explains the odd combination of servility and self-assertion in Mr Collins; how telling it has been to learn a little about his father. The technique thus strengthens the solidity of the characters—even one like Mr Collins who is commonly regarded as a caricature. Novelists often like to surprise us with a twist or two in their tale, but with the paragraphs on Mr Bennet the cleverness is that this novelist does not surprise us at all. The rash marriage to a pretty, lively girl, whose liveliness seemed to be good humour when it was only silliness and the charm of youth; the loss of love and respect for her; the retreat into a world of books and the private, sardonic amusement of the human comedy—we have seen most of this already, we may answer, or have worked it out for ourselves. But there is cunning in this technique: it invites us to acknowledge the roundedness, the sufficiency of the book's characters. The novelist acts first as dramatist and then as critic of her drama.

Very few novelists compose a chapter as Jane Austen composes the first chapter of *Pride and Prejudice*, with the shape and balance of a piece of music. This concern for form extends throughout the book, on both the large scale and the small. The second chapter stands to the first as a kind of response, or 'mirror'. Again it is almost all dialogue, and the topic of conversation is still the new arrival in the neighbourhood, Mr Bingley, but the pattern is inverted in that it is now Mr Bennet who imparts some news to his wife (that he has called on Bingley, who may therefore be expected to pay them a visit). Meanwhile, the author is gradually enlarging her cast, a little like the composer bringing in new instruments one by one. Three of the Bennet daughters were named in the first chapter; now four of them are present (the theatrical method is maintained, in that we learn of their presence only as they are addressed from time to time in the conversation; we do not even know whether Jane, the only daughter unnamed in this chapter, is in the room or not). Meanwhile Bingley is still off-stage and Darcy still unmentioned; they will appear in the third chapter.

The first half of chapter 13 in the first volume is also a mirror of chapter 1. In the first chapter Mrs Bennet told her husband of a new arrival in the neighbourhood; now he performs the same service for her:

> 'I hope, my dear,' said Mr. Bennet to his wife, as they were at breakfast the next morning, 'that you have ordered a good dinner to-day, because I have reason to expect an addition to our family party.'

The straightforward 'said Mr. Bennet to his wife' may serve to bring out the distinctive inflection of ' "Mr. Bennet," said his lady to him' in the earlier scene—that particular piece of archness cannot endure repetition. And the reference to breakfast, sketchy as it is as a piece of scene-setting, may serve to point up the total absence of any setting, in place or time of day, at the book's beginning. The irony in this mirror scene is that Mrs Bennet supposes her husband to be talking about Bingley, whereas he is actually talking about Mr Collins: she supposes the mirror to be supplying a more exact reflection than is actually the case. Form thus becomes itself a kind of wit.

This formal mastery extends throughout the book. For example, two proposals to Elizabeth—from Collins and Darcy—are placed in the centre of the story, contrasted in many ways too obvious to mention, and yet alike as object lessons in how not to propose. In terms of the way in which

the novelist presents them, both these proposals are in turn
contrasted with the second and successful proposal by Darcy.
Whereas the earlier proposals are extended scenes of full-
dress rhetoric, the final proposal is brief, and Elizabeth's
reply is given in indirect speech:[2]

> Elizabeth was too much embarrassed to say a word . . .
> Elizabeth feeling all the more than common awkwardness
> and anxiety of his situation, now forced herself to speak; and
> immediately, though not very fluently, gave him to under-
> stand, that her sentiments had undergone so material a
> change ... [etc.]

The brevity is fitting because the decision, as we know, has
already been made; and the indirect speech is fitting because
Jane Austen is writing subjectively, seeing events through
the medium of the heroine's consciousness; the vagueness of
her account matches Elizabeth's confusion, form agreeing
with content. On the earlier occasions, as in her showdown
with Lady Catherine, she may have been amused, indignant,
or angry, but she has remained essentially master of herself:
she has been able to hear herself. Now, at this moment of
supreme embarrassment and happiness, she can no longer
hear herself, and so we cannot hear her either.

The episode in Derbyshire is a little less brilliant than the
first half of the book, but the later chapters are superbly
designed and told. They are conceived as a series of duets
between the heroine and another character: with Lady
Catherine, with her father, with Darcy, with Jane, with her
father again, and with Darcy again, Elizabeth now reprising
the themes of their earlier duet, rather seriously presented
then but now ornamented with playful, sprightly humour.
Diverse in character, these encounters are nonetheless all in

the comic mode, except for a short instant when Mr Bennet is trying to dissuade his daughter from marrying Darcy: ' "My child, let me not have the grief of seeing *you* unable to respect your partner in life." '[3] This marvellous and terrible moment is perhaps the emotional high point of the entire book, though so short that it can be missed (it was altogether fluffed in the recent BBC adaptation). Is there a better example anywhere of the power of italics?—three letters only. Briefly, Mr Bennet half drops the mask, and reveals the deadness of his marriage, the emotional emptiness of his life. And he reveals something more: the long, unspoken understanding between himself and his favourite daughter. He despises his wife. He knows that Elizabeth knows; and he knows that she knows that he knows. In a sense these few words 'redeem' Mr Bennet, for they discover that there is, after all, one person whom he cares about deeply, but in a sense not, for he has the self-knowledge to realize that he will always retreat rapidly from emotional openness (when Elizabeth urged him not to be too severe with himself over Lydia's disgrace, he replied, with the blend of self-reproach, self-knowledge, and saturnine wit that is so distinctively his own, 'No, Lizzy, let me once in my life feel how much I have been to blame. I am not afraid of being overpowered by the impression. It will pass soon enough').[4] Almost any other writer, having conceived Mr Bennet's oblique confession to his daughter, would have milked it for its pathos, but it is right that it should be momentary, both in terms of the genre to which this novel belongs, that of easy romantic comedy, and in terms of Mr Bennet's character. With masterly restraint, Jane Austen allows the cloud to obscure the sun for only a few seconds; by the end of the scene—which is itself not long —the mask has been replaced, and Mr Bennet is his usual, sardonically amusing self. Virginia Woolf once said about Jane Austen that 'of all great writers she is the most difficult to catch in the act of greatness'. It is quite false: there is hardly another novelist of whom one may so readily say, 'That chapter, that paragraph, that sentence is a moment of genius.'

The technique of novel-writing is one of Jane Austen's themes in *Northanger Abbey*; she points out, for example, how the physical form of the book prevents the novelist from concealing how near she is to the conclusion of her story (readers 'will see in the tell-tale compression of the pages before them, that we are all hastening together to perfect felicity').[5] How is the novelist to get background information to the reader without obvious clumsiness? *Northanger Abbey* has some good if slightly juvenile fun with that problem too ('This brief account of the family is intended to supersede the necessity of a long and minute detail from Mrs. Thorpe herself, of her past adventures and sufferings, which might otherwise be expected to occupy the three or four following chapters; in which the worthlessness of lords and attornies might be set forth, and conversations, which had passed twenty years before, be minutely repeated').[6] On the first page of *Persuasion* Jane Austen solves this problem, with a bravura display of technique: she lays out the basic information about her main characters in a way that is drily factual and yet at the same time a brilliant piece of satire at Sir Walter Elliot's expense. We should realize that she is exulting in the sheer ingenuity of her performance, and an enjoyment of that virtuosity is a proper part of our own aesthetic pleasure.

In the case of *Pride and Prejudice* the author's self-conscious mastery of technique is exhibited supremely in the plot. Coleridge once said that the three most perfect plots ever planned were *Oedipus Tyrannus, The Alchemist,* and *Tom Jones*; he might have added *Pride and Prejudice* to that list. Its plot is a superb piece of machinery, and as with a Rolls-Royce, part of the proper pleasure that we take in the book lies in our appreciation of the quality of the engineering and the smoothness of the ride. It is worth taking the machinery apart to see how it is put together. The finest plots can be divided into two classes, the simple and the complex. The *Iliad* is a supreme example of a simple plot: its action, which has no subplots, moves forward with a clear, inexorable logic. *Pride and Prejudice* is, like *Tom Jones,* a masterpiece of complex plotting: its especial beauty lies in the craft with which the primary plot and the various subplots are woven together.

There are four stories of courtship and marriage: the history of Elizabeth and Darcy, and as subplots Jane and Bingley, Lydia and Wickham, Charlotte and Mr Collins. The hero and heroine are each connected to each of these subplots by a different route (Elizabeth is the sister of Jane and Lydia, the friend of Charlotte; Darcy is the friend of Bingley, and related to the patrons of both Wickham and Collins). The enmity between Darcy and Wickham might be classified as another subplot. These five plots are interlinked with exemplary skill, the crucial mechanism being the admission of two coincidences: that Darcy and Wickham, for quite separate reasons, should turn up in the same part of the country at the same time; and that the heir on whom the Bennets' property is entailed, Mr Collins, should happen to be the protégé of Darcy's aunt. We should not regard the use of coincidence as a flaw: on the contrary, this is just how a novel of manners ought to be—an essentially naturalistic situation given shape and neatness by the sort of coincidences that do occur from time to time in real life. Much of what happens in common life just happens—it does not make a story; but some of the events of common life do. It is not a story that a bored young man is taken by the liveliness of a pretty young woman; it is not a story that a lively young woman takes against a snooty young man; the charm of *Pride and Prejudice* is to narrate how, because of a couple of perfectly plausible coincidences, such ordinary occurrences became the basis of a story worth the telling. (In *Emma*, by a different kind of ingenuity, when the requirements of the plot demand a not especially likely turn of events, Jane Austen turns potential awkwardness to advantage: Mr Knightley observes bitterly that Frank Churchill is indeed the child of fortune: events always seem to go his way, and when it suits him for his aunt and adoptive mother to die, she obligingly does so.[7])

I have compared *Pride and Prejudice* to a Rolls-Royce, but the metaphor is imperfect. This novel is a wonderful machine, but for sheer skill and smoothness in the progression of the story and the development of the characters' experience *Mansfield Park* and *Emma* are superior even to *Pride and Prejudice*. And there are some small awkwardnesses in the working out of the complex plot. The most obvious comes in Darcy's angry letter to Elizabeth: it is hard to believe that a man of his character would have been prepared to reveal, and on paper, his sister's shame.[8] But the plot requires it, and plausibility must yield for a moment to plot.

Does it matter? Sophocles' *Oedipus Tyrannus* has always been recognized as one of the greatest plots; yet notoriously it contains several gross implausibilities. The difference between this play and *Pride and Prejudice* is of course that the latter is naturalistic, so that the reader may in this case be intolerant of improbabilities that he would accept without demur in heroic drama. We can, I think, see Jane Austen trying to get over the (rather small) difficulty that her plot has given her: she asks us to understand the complexity of Darcy's state of mind—under the pressure of frustration and humiliation he is indeed acting 'out of character'. In his self-analysis near the end of the book he looks back at this time: '"When I wrote that letter," replied Darcy, "I believed myself perfectly calm and cool, but I am since convinced that it was written in a dreadful bitterness of spirit."'[9] It is that bitter and passionate compulsion to justify himself that leads him to reveal to Elizabeth what he would otherwise keep a secret. Perhaps that is not totally convincing as an explanation, but it comes pretty close. There is a meticulousness about Jane Austen's craftsmanship that makes her want to mend even the smallest imperfections; and that fact is more striking than the imperfections themselves. A few years ago, I read in succession three novels in which the denouement was brought about by a car crash. Jane Austen would not have allowed herself so arbitrary or easy a mechanism. The off-stage death of Frank's aunt in *Emma* is not arbitrary. She has been in poor health from the moment that we first heard of her. Her death is not in fact essential to the plot: it would have been easy enough to find another way of freeing Frank to marry Jane Fairfax. And the death has a moral significance, bringing out the jealousy which the virtuous

Mr Knightley cannot quite contain ('"His aunt is in the way.—His aunt dies . . .—He is a fortunate young man indeed."').

In many novels—including some of the very best—we may feel that the business of wrapping up the plot is more of a challenge to the author than a pleasure. His denouement may be competent, even skilful, he may make appropriate gestures of closure (Jane Austen makes some jokes about such processes at the end of *Northanger Abbey*), yet one may sense that this is not where the writer's heart is. But in *Pride and Prejudice*, which is all plot and all wit, the wit enters the plot itself: it is a hilarious part of the unravelling that Lady Catherine's very attempt to prevent Darcy's engagement to Elizabeth is what precipitates his proposal. Lizzy herself laughs about the plot: 'Lady Catherine has been of infinite use, which ought to make her happy, for she loves to be of use.'[10]

This tempts me into a digression—which may, in fact, tell us a little about Jane Austen's art. 'Who Betrays Elizabeth Bennet?' is the essay which provides the title for one of John Sutherland's collections of literary puzzles. How is it, Sutherland asks, that Lady Catherine has heard a rumour of Elizabeth's impending engagement, when no one else seems to know about it? Elizabeth's own supposition is that since she and Jane are sisters and Darcy and Bingley close friends, the excitement about one wedding has made everybody eager to supply the idea of another. Sutherland calls this 'a weak supposition—unworthy of the sharp-witted Miss Bennet'. His own answer is that Mrs Collins, the former Charlotte Lucas, has fed the story to Lady Catherine from jealousy of Elizabeth: she calculates (wrongly, as it

17

transpires) that Lady Catherine will provoke from Elizabeth an outburst against Darcy that will put him off for good.

This suggestion may be a tease, with a second possibility implied: that for reasons of plot Jane Austen has needed Lady Catherine to hear the rumour, but not found a plausible way of getting it to her. At all events, Sutherland's solution is in fact ruled out by the author's description of Charlotte as 'really rejoicing at the match'; she is last seen on a visit to her parents, enjoying the newly betrothed Elizabeth's company.[11] And actually the book does unobtrusively explain how the rumour reached Rosings. Mr Collins's letter to Mr Bennet congratulating him on Jane's engagement indicates that he has had the news from what Mr Bennet calls 'some of the good-natured, gossiping Lucases' and goes on to declare that the rumour of Elizabeth's impending engagement comes from 'the same authority'.[12] So the Lucases have told their son-in-law, and he will inevitably have passed the tidings on to his patroness.

This creates an agreeable irony, which Jane Austen may have consciously designed. Earlier in the story Sir William has seemed amiably obtuse in pressing Darcy and Elizabeth on one another against their wishes, but in a sense he will prove to have been the first person to 'get it right' ('Mr. Darcy, you must allow me to present this young lady to you as a very desirable partner').[13] And now the silly old Lucases have been innocent enough to fancy that Lizzy and Darcy too will be getting engaged soon, while any worldly-wise person, like clever Mr Bennet, will see how absurd the idea is. But destiny has hidden the truth from the wise and revealed it to babes, and the Lucases, like Lady Catherine herself, have unwittingly done more to push the business on to its happy conclusion than they could have imagined. Of course, it is true that Jane Austen has devised the Lucases' bit of gossip for plot reasons, but it is interesting both that she has troubled to devise an answer to a problem that would not occur to one of her readers in a thousand, and that the answer should have its own piquancy. It is interesting not least because another pretty obvious expedient is open to her. A man desperately in love is not likely to be able to conceal his feelings altogether, and indeed when Miss Bingley criticizes Elizabeth at Pemberley, Darcy retorts that he considers her not merely pretty but one of the handsomest women of his acquaintance.[14] Jane Austen could have saved Sutherland his question by indicating that someone in Darcy's circle had warned Lady Catherine of the danger; that would have been easy enough, but it would have been less amusing.

2

The Shape of Comedy

The strength of her plots as structures enables Jane Austen to dispense with the melodramatic or outlandish incidents that appear in most of the novels written by her contemporaries. Complaining about the absence of factory chimneys and the events of the Napoleonic War from her books is now out of fashion, and rightly so. It is no more deplorable for her not to mention Napoleon than it is for Defoe's Moll Flanders never to notice that there is a civil war on: in each case the matter is simply not pertinent to the sort of story that the author wants to tell. Jane Austen seems to provide little 'background' in her novels; but as it happens, her grounding in reality and sense of significant detail are so firm that we learn more from her about social and cultural texture and habits of life in her time—teenage girls lunching together at an inn, what a bookish young lady is likely to be reading in 1809, how naval officers dispose of themselves when peace breaks out—than we do from other novelists of the day. But we hear about these things only when they bear upon her story. She once told her niece Anna, who had been trying her hand at fiction, that her descriptions of place were 'often more minute than will be liked', with 'too many particulars of right hand and of left'.[1] It is advice that should be more often heeded, especially in our own time, when too many novelists substitute the multiplication of descriptive detail for that seizure of the *petit fait signicatif* which Stendhal, more wisely, saw as the novelist's task.

Jane Austen's is a chastened art. Her instinct to purify and concentrate tells her to keep the scenery to a minimum. That same instinct leads her to resist the proliferation of minor characters; for example, she dispenses with the comic servant who chunters his way through so much of eighteenth- and nineteenth-century fiction. It is significant, too, that there is even less overtly dramatic incident in her later novels than in her earlier work: she does develop her range in these later books, not, as we might have expected, by taking obviously bigger themes, but through yet more intimacy and refinement. They become even more 'ordinary'. We can appreciate from the books themselves how deliberately their modesty of incident is designed, but there is evidence outside them which confirms it.

For the real life around Jane Austen was a good deal more dramatic than the imaginary world that she created. Sudden death, which has essentially no part in her books (Mrs Churchill, in *Emma*, had been long ill; Dr Grant's death in *Mansfield Park*, treated comically and dispatched in less than half a sentence, is effectively outside the action of the novel), was part of common experience: Jane's sister-in-law, her brother James's first wife, was taken ill unexpectedly, and died the same day. Her aunt by marriage, Mrs Leigh Perrot, faced greater vicissitudes than any of her heroines. Born in Barbados, she was sent to England to be educated at the age of 6; separated from a beloved brother, she never saw him again. In her mid-fifties she was indicted for grand larceny, faced transportation had she not been acquitted, and even so spent several months of imprisonment while awaiting trial, the privations of a Georgian gaol being only partly mitigated by the privileges which money could buy. More romantic and poignant was Jane's first cousin Eliza Hancock, born in India, possibly the natural daughter of Warren Hastings. Pretty, witty, and good-natured, she married a French count, who was guillotined in the Terror. Back in London she struggled to look after her sickly son, an only child who died at the age of 15. She was married again, to Jane's brother Henry, but died painfully of cancer. Now there was someone much more obviously 'born to be a heroine' than any of the actual leading ladies in Jane Austen's books.

Her heroes come from what seem to be immemorially stable gentry families. But as Claire Tomalin shows in her biography, some of the prosperous landowners in that part of Hampshire where Jane Austen grew up were a good deal more mobile and richly coloured.[2] A couple of local peers were not the aristocrats one might have supposed, but new creations. Lord Bolton, who received his title in 1795, was a north-countryman of very modest origins who had come into money by marrying the bastard daughter of a duke. Lord Dorchester was an Irishman who had done brilliantly as a soldier in Canada, and prudently by finding an earl's daughter for his wife. Far more extraordinary was the Earl of Portsmouth. As a child, a few years before Jane Austen's birth, he had spent a few months under her parents' roof as a pupil at the little school that they ran from their parsonage, and been the playmate of their elder children. But he grew disturbed in mind, and by the end of his twenties had developed a lively interest in sadism and necrophilia, and one that was not merely theoretical. When he was 32, his brothers married him off to a woman fifteen years his senior: she presumably found the title of countess worth the sacrifice, while they wanted to prevent him producing a legitimate heir. After her death a wicked lawyer forced him into a marriage with his daughter; the new countess, abetted by an accomplice, instituted a reign of terror, whipping and torturing her husband, who was not rescued from this horror until nine years had passed, whereupon the villains sank into disgrace and poverty. This bizarre history was some way beyond Catherine Morland's most Gothic imaginings. So Jane Austen could, if she had chosen, have made her own stories more dramatic—even melodramatic—while remaining, in the strict sense, 'true to life'. The mildness of incident in her books, and the absence of farouche characters, is a matter of discipline and conscious choice

The appetite of Jane's admirers for the details of her life and background has meant that the Austens have fortuitously found themselves perhaps the most intensely studied small gentry family of the time in England. Their tale is interesting for the light that it sheds on social history, but it may also help us to understand the world about which Jane Austen wrote and some realities that her first readers took for granted. The Austens were in origin tradesmen in Kent who made money and lifted themselves into the lower reaches of gentility. But for complicated reasons to do with deaths and problems with wills the early life of George

Austen, Jane's father, was difficult and insecure. However, he got himself to Oxford and into a college fellowship; luckily, he was handsome and married well. His sister exported herself to India in the hope of picking up a husband there, and married a man much older than herself; it is her daughter who may have been fathered by Warren Hastings. Jane's mother, Cassandra Leigh, came of more aristocratic stock. The family seat, Stoneleigh Abbey, is a baroque mansion of palatial size. There was a barony in the family, and Jane was also related through the Leighs to at least two other peers; her great-great-uncle, the Duke of Chandos, had been one of the highest noblemen in the realm. But grand connections did not mean grand living, and she and her parents were short of money for most of their lives. Nonetheless, these links to the high aristocracy give a significance to the fact that there are no noblemen in her novels (Lady Catherine de Bourgh is a nobleman's daughter, and there is a peer in the abandoned fragment, *The Watsons*): that is another kind of factitious glamour which she deliberately avoids.

The same fluidity can be seen if we trace the fortunes of her brothers' descendants. From her eldest brother James, regarded in his youth as the literary one of the family, comes a dynasty of clergymen, dons, and civil servants, with a least one author of a published book in each of the next five generations; this branch of the family provides us with almost all the information we have about Jane, outside her own letters and writings. Another brother, Edward, who was adopted by a rich childless couple called Knight, rose into the upper gentry and became 'county', with grand houses in both Kent and Hampshire. Such splendour could not be sustained through the twentieth century; Chawton

House, in the shadow of which the novelist spent her last years, has been let on long lease to a Californian Janeite, who has established there a centre for the study of women's writing. Francis was the more successful of the two sailor brothers, rising to a knighthood and the exalted height of an Admiral of the Fleet. Charles, despite ending with an admiral's rank, had a life dogged with misfortune; some of his descendants continued upper middle-class, but one of his great-grandsons became a grocer's assistant, another a bricklayer. Jane Austen understood such social flux: her women may have the chance to make a brilliant match, but they also face the danger of penurious spinsterhood, and if they attract a suitor who is below them in the social scale, they may have to weigh the odds and decide whether to accept or hold out for the uncertain chance of something better. Except perhaps for *Northanger Abbey*, that anxiety swims beneath the surface of all her books, even *Pride and Prejudice*.

There is little gratitude in literary criticism: Jane Austen's plots are so well made and her episodes so natural that she is liable to be reproached for tiny flaws which would excite no comment in the case of almost any other novelist. And *Pride and Prejudice* seems so perfect a comedy that it appears almost to be a matter of professional pride in some critics to find something wrong with it somewhere. Thus the subplot concerning Wickham—his scheme to seduce Miss Darcy and elope with her, partly for the sake of her fortune—has been found fault with as too crude for this novel's delicate texture. Yet such things were surely not uncommon. Jane Austen's fault here, if such it is, lies in being not too melo-dramatic but too conventional.

Claire Tomalin also objects that Wickham's character seems unconvincing: from what we see of him he appears to be merely frivolous rather than a cold-hearted villain.[3] A possible response to this criticism is to say that it denies the most basic datum about Wickham: the whole point of him is that he appears charming, and that even when one sees through the charm, he still appears not much worse than feckless and sponging—but the reality is more sinister. This deceptiveness in Wickham would seem to be part of the novel's earliest conception: it is the pivot upon which the entire plot turns. True, the fact that something is a basic datum of a novel, or the kernel around which the rest of the book has grown, does not absolve the novelist from making it convincing. A good case in point is *Tess of the D'Urbervilles*. That Tess murders her lover and swings for it was Hardy's starting point, based upon an actual case. But it remains an uncomfortable fact that in the book as written Tess's act of murder seems inadequately motivated and her flight and death an awkward appendage to the story; all this feels like a forced attempt to wrench the plot factitiously into the shape of tragedy. This fault in the book cannot be defended either by noting that Tess's execution was the original seed from which the book grew or by observing that the *crime passionel*, foolish and needless, has sometimes been a fact of life.

Similarly, if Jane Austen has failed to make Wickham plausibly nasty, it is an imperfect defence to say that it is a datum of the book that his nastiness should be implausible. It is perhaps half a defence: the basic conception of Wickham is of a charming conman, and if a reader finds him feckless rather than crafty and calculating, one is tempted to reply that he has succeeded yet again in what he does so well—in conning you. But there are two other things which can be said in the author's support. The first is that we do not actually know for sure how wicked Wickham is. Darcy lays some weight upon malice and cruelty as among Wickham's motives for the attempted seduction of his sister, but Darcy is not an objective judge. Jane Austen has the artistry to give a sense of complexity of motives even in the actions of a subsidiary character; but since Wickham is indeed a subsidiary character, whose function within the novel is to be seen through other people's eyes, we do not need to know, or even speculate much, about the balance between those motives.

The other point to be made takes us towards the heart of Jane Austen's moral imagination. She is constantly aware, throughout her works, of the nearness of evil to the comfortable social surface. She knows that the socially acceptable sins—what our own age often calls peccadilloes—may be truly cruel and vicious, and are not the less so for being common. Henry Crawford is the most obvious case (as well as the most complex, since he is a man with the capacity to admire virtue and the possibility of attaining it): he has utterly ruined at least one life, and gravely wounded several others, and yet Jane Austen is truthful in noting that the world will barely censure him: 'That punishment, the public punishment of disgrace, should in a just measure attend *his* share of the offence, is, we know, not one of the barriers, which society gives to virtue.'[4] We may be certain that Wickham's intended crime, the seduction of an impressionable adolescent with a great deal of money, would very soon have made her miserable, and caused much other distress. It would have been indeed a wicked act, and yet its successful execution would not have brought about social disgrace;

perhaps, on the contrary, an entrée into good society. Wickham is not an implausible character; and Jane Austen is not wrong to be harsh with him.

There are good, even great novelists who are not good story-tellers, and there are highly gifted story-tellers who write thoroughly bad books. Jane Austen was a very good story-teller and a very good novelist. How did she do it? Was it all due to native talent? Or did she need to serve an apprenticeship to her craft, to learn from experience, and from the example of other writers?

Her career does indeed present us with a central and probably insoluble mystery. We know that in her early twenties she wrote first versions of the novels which eventually became *Northanger Abbey* (then called *Susan*; the present title is not hers), *Sense and Sensibility* (then called *Elinor and Marianne*), and *Pride and Prejudice* (then called *First Impressions*). It was ten years or so before she returned to these manuscripts and revised or recast them. How radically did she change them? Some biographers suppose that the earlier versions were essentially the books that we have today. Jane Austen is indeed an extraordinary phenomenon on any account, but if they are right, as they may be, we are faced with one of the most astonishing occurrences in all literary history. *Pride and Prejudice* is perhaps as perfect a comedy of manners as was ever written in prose. *Sense and Sensibility*, that jagged, imperfect, and deeply poignant book, contains in its second chapter what remains perhaps the most sustainedly savage passage of satire in English literature. We thus face the possibility that prose fiction which matched and in some respects even surpassed anything that anyone had produced anywhere was written by a very young woman with rather slight education and very little knowledge of the world, and that these masterpieces then sat, unknown, in a country vicarage for a decade and more. A very few poets and composers have achieved greatness even in their teens, but it is hard to think of another novelist who has flown so high so early.

However, although her development in her twenties is mysterious, we know more about her fledgling efforts than is the case with most novelists. James Austen, Jane's eldest brother, and his descendants combined strong family feeling with literary and scholarly interests, with the result that her juvenilia have survived, some the products of her adolescence, while others may date from a quite early childhood. Such a survival is so rare and these pieces are so much fun that it is tempting to make too much of them. If they were less rare—if we were reading the childish efforts of Dickens or Tolstoy—we might be better placed to know how significant it is that they are in some ways so unlike her mature works. In one sense they show us that she was very precocious: there is hardly any teenage prose which has been read with so much pleasure. Yet one may still feel about them as one does about the star turn at the school concert: part of our genuine pleasure in the performance is the consciousness that the performer is remarkably good for her age. With *The Young Visiters* Daisy Ashford produced at the age of 9 what is perhaps the only literary masterpiece written by a child. And at the age of 14 Tennyson wrote *The Devil and the Lady,* an astonishingly mature pastiche of Elizabethan drama (and strikingly unlike his adult verse). These works, in their very different ways, were prodigious; in contrast, the teenage Jane Austen was very bright, but she was not a prodigy.

Her juvenilia are nonetheless impressive—and surprising. For they reveal a boisterous, hoydenish, sometimes surreal imagination; they are immensely high-spirited, anarchic, occasionally violent in a cartoonish way, and often hilariously funny. The comparisons that they prompt are with Sterne, Edward Lear, Ionesco, or Monty Python, rather than George Eliot or Henry James. That might suggest how self-conscious is the chastened surface of her mature work—or rather, we may feel, as we look closer, that the exuberance is still there as a potentiality kept in check, with the suppressed energy of a coiled spring. It is certainly wrong to see her as wild in the sense of being a social or emotional rebel (that is even worse than painting her as a conservative ideologue), but her formal self-control does not mean that her content is always comparably restrained. Miss Bates is almost Dickensian. Some viewers of the BBC *Pride and Prejudice* thought Alison Stedman's portrayal of Mrs Bennet overdone—and went back to the book only to find that those extravagances were all there in the text. The dainty porcelain idea of Miss Austen was swept away a long time ago, but perhaps we find it difficult to rid our heads of it entirely.

There is an attraction, then, in seeing her as a person of naturally exuberant, even wild imagination whose novels are created through the tight disciplining of a natural ebullience. Yet this is only a partial truth. The child's imagination is different from the adult's, and the fact that the childishness of Jane's early scribbles is so brilliant and endearing does not necessarily mean that her later imagination would have stayed wacky unless she had chastened it.

There is a case for seeing her spontaneous development as having been in more or less the opposite direction—towards naturalism. Some evidence for this comes from the fragmentary *Lesley Castle*. Written about a year and a half after *Love and Freindship*, it resembles that larky *jeu d'esprit* in being told through letters and also in being planned, by the look of it, as parody-farce. One of the correspondents, Miss Charlotte Luttrell, is given an obsession with food. At first this is wholly and extravagantly grotesque, but it evolves into a portrayal of comic character more like those of Dickens—or like Mrs Bennet or Miss Bates. Meanwhile, the story, what there is of it, is growing somewhat more 'serious' and naturalistic, and, to be frank, a little dull. Jane no doubt saw that the thing had become a mess, and abandoned it. But what remains interesting is the germ of a new, more naturalistic kind of comedy and story-telling—evolving, it would appear, of itself, without much previous design.

A similar moral can be drawn from *Northanger Abbey*, in its origins apparently the earliest of the novels. A pleasure and a flaw of this book is that its protagonist is too good for her purpose. No one, says her creator, would have supposed Catherine Morland born to be a heroine,[5] and at the start of the book we might suppose her born to be a butt. Planned, it might seem, to be a kind of female Candide, she insists on turning into someone more like Sophia Western. Though naive, she is animated, persistent, open, and warm-hearted, with a pleasing touch of obstinacy ('But Catherine could be stubborn too').[6] If this were Jane Austen's only novel, Catherine would be celebrated as one of the most charming heroines in English fiction. 'Is there a Henry in the world who could be insensible to such a declaration?' the author exclaims, after Catherine's most touching effusion of artless agitation.[7] Any writer who tells us that her characters are delightful takes a risk, but Jane Austen gets away with it here, because she is right. But the consequence is that the semi-farcical part of the plot—Catherine's suspecting dark mysteries hidden in the furniture, and persuading herself that General Tilney has made away with his wife—comes to jar a little. The story requires her to be silly, and we have got to know her well enough to think that she is not as silly as that. Jane Austen has to work round the difficulty, by representing Catherine's fantasies as momentary lapses: she is ashamed of her foolishness about the chest and the cupboard, and when Henry detects her suspicions of the General, she is suffused with an agonizing and thoroughly believable sense of embarrassment and shame. But a small awkwardness remains: the episode of the secret message in the cupboard is the only place in the novels where the action itself is parodic—where the author makes one of her characters behave as she does in order to send up another author—in this case Mrs Radcliffe in *The Mysteries of Udolpho*. It looks as though she may have planned a less naturalistic novel, but her talent for the creation of believable characters pushed the book in a more naturalistic direction—as it were, further from *Love and Freindship* and closer to *Pride and Prejudice*.

A glance at her earliest writings is one way of meeting the question, 'Where does Jane Austen's art come from?' Another, of course, is to look at the writers who preceded or were contemporary with her and to examine what she may have learnt from them. But the chief result of this exercise is to show how strikingly unlike she was to any other novelists of her time. Jane Austen is often seen as a conservative genius, a writer who brought unusual refinement and perception to conventional forms and themes; in reality, she was notably original in form and technique. But in one respect she was indeed conspicuously unadventurous: all her novels follow the simple pattern 'girl meets boy, girl marries boy'. Even *Lady Susan*, with a wicked and older woman for its principal character, has the theme of the virtuous girl getting her man as its denouement. The sixty or so existing pages of *Sanditon* mostly study the growth of a new town and its inhabitants; but insofar as Jane Austen had a clear notion of where this book was to go, it too was evidently to be built around a young woman eventually marrying the man of her heart.

'Boy meets girl, boy gets girl' is one of the most basic and universal story patterns that one can imagine, and Jane Austen uses only one of its many subspecies: that in which the story is seen from the woman's point of view. Cinderella is another example of this subspecies, though, as we shall see, most of Jane Austen's heroines are not quite the Cinderella type. Part of her effect lies in the counterpoint between the archetypal simplicity of the underlying pattern and the sophistication of what is built upon it. A sense of the archetype's simplicity may also help us to appreciate the subtlety with which she varies the basic pattern. These are variations both of form and ethos; indeed part of her art, at its most assured, is to use formal variation as a means of making ethos.

Thus the distinctive feature of *Pride and Prejudice* is the number of its subplots, knit into one another with confident mastery. The abundance of anecdote and episode in the book—the sheer amount of things happening—is a part of its vitality; it is a means of imparting the ethos of sparkling comedy. At the same time the making of the story matches the character of its heroine. The narrative is energetic, resourceful, lively, delighting in its own wit and skill—all characteristics of Lizzy Bennet herself. This is not to say that the book is bland, or ignorant of cruelty and ruthlessness. The marriages of Mr Bennet and Charlotte Lucas, for example, might in another novel—even in another novel by Jane Austen, like *Mansfield Park*—have had their emptiness more lengthily and painfully exposed; the bitterness and savagery of the competition between Mrs Bennet and her neighbours for social advantage and success in the marriage market might have been etched with the needle of a more acid satire. Lizzy Bennet's own view of human nature is black indeed: she assumes that their acquaintance will exult in her family's disgrace—'under such a misfortune as this, one cannot see too little of one's neighbours ... Let them triumph over us at a distance'—just as she assumes that Darcy would triumph if he knew how badly she now wants him.[8] Besides, the author confirms in her own voice that the neighbourhood delighted in Lydia's shame and was disappointed that it was not worse, though the 'spiteful old ladies in Meryton' could console themselves that, with Wickham for a husband, her misery was certain.[9] None of the later novels to the same degree displays to us culture red in tooth and claw. But *Pride and Prejudice* is a true triumph of the comic spirit—of deep comedy, rising from the heart of human life—because it knows about these things, and is undeceived, and yet allows the pleasures of comedy and celebration to subordinate them. The book does not assert that life is a jest (Mr Bennet says that it is, but he decidedly does not speak for the author);

the triumph of comedy within it is a triumph of form. It takes one element in human life, and enjoys it. How large a part of human life that element is, the book does not need to say.

Whereas *Pride and Prejudice* establishes its comic character on the very first page, *Sense and Sensibility* begins more sombrely, as though Elinor and Marianne were being prepared to go through the romantic vicissitudes of the typical heroine of an eighteenth-century novel, and the second chapter, as I have already noted, is unsurpassed in English literature as a set-piece of sustained satiric savagery. The tone and ethos of these two books, written at similar periods in their author's career, is profoundly different. The most obvious variant on the basic story pattern in *Sense and Sensibility* is that two girls meet two boys. This sets up certain expectations of symmetry or contrast that in a way are met, in a way not. We expect either Sense to triumph over Sensibility, or a final and mature balance between the two to be achieved; in the event, neither of these things quite happens. We might perhaps conceive of a happy ending for one heroine (Elinor, through whose eyes the action is mostly seen) and an unhappy ending for the other; more probably, we expect each heroine to achieve her happy ending in the form of a happy marriage. This both does and does not happen. Marianne's marriage is felt in some way as a defeat; and if it becomes fully and deeply happy, it becomes so only a considerable time after the book's closure, in a future beyond the narrative.

Such half-fulfilments of symmetry and half-frustrations of expectation are part of what makes this book so interestingly angular. My own belief is that Jane Austen purposely designed it to be troubling and difficult, whereas by contrast

Pride and Prejudice is all confidence and ease. But it must be conceded that the awkwardness within *Sense and Sensibility* cannot all be attributed to an aesthetic and a moral standpoint which have been consciously chosen; the author does not seem to have the working-out of her story perfectly under control. A common view is that she started with a scheme (roughly, Sense right, Sensibility wrong) which proved in the end too rigid; on this account, *Sense and Sensibility* belongs with such works as *Così fan tutte,* Trimalchio's dinner in Petronius, and perhaps *The Merchant of Venice,* where we can see, or may suspect, that the creator's imaginative vitality has overridden a formally or morally simple scheme to produce something more complex and ambivalent. In other words, Jane Austen has wanted Marianne to be proved wrong, but has made her too poignant and sympathetic for us to accept that judgement. Later in this essay I shall suggest a different view: not that the book tries to refute Sensibility and fails, but that the flaw lies elsewhere.

One variant of the 'girl meets boy' pattern in *Mansfield Park* and *Persuasion* is that girl has already met boy before the main narrative begins, and in each case, though in different ways, this variation imparts a certain sobriety of tone. A peculiar subtlety of *Mansfield Park* is that what is normally the denouement of the story and often the major part of the action—girl and boy get together—is excluded from the main narrative: it is turned into a postscript to the main action, as part of the final chapter of winding up, and the author explicitly refuses to describe it. Fanny, like all the heroines, gets her happy ending at last, but the formal structure is such that this novel, uniquely in the canon, is hardly a comedy at all. Fanny has won a pyrrhic victory: she has defeated Mary Crawford, but the battlefield is strewn with bodies: Edmund, Sir Thomas—anyone we care about is wrecked and wretched. Only the passage of time—the future, described in the last chapter, which has the character of an epilogue—will be able, imperfectly, to heal the wounds.

In *Emma* too girl has met boy before the story begins, but here the variant is of course that girl does not realize that she has met the destined boy until late in the action. This heroine also varies a classic story pattern in that she is an inverted Cinderella: she starts 'rich, handsome and clever' and seems to have nowhere to go but down. *Emma* is arguably the only one of the novels in which we might suspect that the heroine may not end well (even in *Mansfield Park* I think we know that Fanny will get a man—we may not be sure which man—because otherwise the story has nowhere to go). The principal characters in the book include three marriageable women (Emma, Harriet Smith, and Jane Fairfax) and three marriageable men (Knightley, Elton, and Frank Churchill). When Mr Elton 'breaks the rules' by importing a wife from outside the narrative, there are left only two men for three women. True, Harriet has been interested in Robert Martin, but he is soon (surely?) out of contention. That is apparently confirmed when Harriet says, 'I hope I know better now, than to care for Mr. Martin, or to be suspected of it.'[10] That seems pretty decisive: we are bound to agree that someone who has once felt as Harriet now does about Knightley cannot contentedly go back to the yeoman farmer.

And there is another, formal reason for supposing that Robert Martin is out of the running. At the very end of *Northanger Abbey*, Jane Austen marries Eleanor Tilney off to a rich lord who has never been heard of before, and mischievously observing that the rules of composition forbid her to introduce a new character into the story not connected with the plot, concocts an absurd and flimsy link to relate him to the earlier action. The 'rules of composition' encourage us not to take account of Robert Martin. He is not quite one of the dramatis personae: Emma sees him at one point, but neither speaks to him nor hears him speak. On the other hand, not only does Robert Martin remain in love with Harriet but there are occasional hints at intervals through the book that she has not cast him off as irrevocably as might appear. The author's purpose is not so much clearly to deceive us, in the manner of Agatha Christie, as to leave us puzzled.

It is interesting to compare and contrast the plot of Maria Edgeworth's *Belinda*. In *Emma* there appears to be one woman too many; in *Belinda* there is an extra man. Early in the story a man is introduced who is signalled as the one whom the heroine ought to marry. But later another virtuous lover appears, and Belinda becomes engaged to him. How then is the happy ending to be achieved? The author has boxed herself into a corner, and her only way out is to invent a grave moral flaw which develops in the second lover, justifying Belinda in breaking the engagement. It is transparently artificial, and at odds with anything that has gone before; here is an author whose plot has escaped her control. It may look as though Jane Austen has similarly boxed herself, or perhaps her heroine, into a corner: either Emma must lose Knightley or bear the guilt of wrecking Harriet's happiness. In fact, as we all know, she is in perfect command of her story, and breaks free with the ease of a

Houdini. It seems likely that almost no one now reads this book without knowing beforehand how it will end, and that is a pity: it becomes harder to appreciate the author's teasing manipulations. *Emma* is a great comedy, but it gets some of its edge and its eventual exhilaration from the way in which it seems to come close to developing in a darker direction.

D. W. Harding said that Jane Austen was fascinated by the Cinderella theme.[11] This is a half-truth, for her cunning is to present us with an aspect of this archetypal story and then to put it to one side: she is the master of the archetype, not in thrall to it. In *Persuasion* Anne Elliot is the neglected one of three sisters. On the other hand, she is socially the grandest of the heroines, the only one whose father has a handle to his name, and the Cinderella motif works well here, because it is paradoxical: even though Sir Walter has had to retrench, she still lives elegantly, and Anne's servitude to her 'ugly sisters' is emotional rather than literal. Essential to the Cinderella story is the combination of two elements: the girl is neglected; and she makes a dazzling marriage. None of Jane Austen's heroines fits this story pattern, and most of them exhibit neither of these two elements. Fanny Price is neglected, she is separated from her natural parents, and her relationship to her cousins Maria and Julia is stepsisterly. She begins, that is to say, in Cinderella's situation, but she does not make a glamorous marriage: she weds, as his second choice, her first cousin, a dull clergyman who, as a younger son, will not be rich. If we want a fairy-tale archetype for *Pride and Prejudice*, it might better be found in Beauty and the Beast: Elizabeth gives her love to the man who has seemed morally ugly to everyone before his transformation. Of course, Darcy makes a paradoxical version of the Beast, as he is strikingly handsome in appearance. But certainly Elizabeth Bennet is no Cinderella. Although she is the only one of the heroines to marry distinctly well, she has suffered no neglect. She is of a lively and happy disposition, and has the most emotionally secure background of any of the heroines (she is, incidentally, the only one to have both parents fully functioning in the action of the story); not only do older people praise her looks, but two young men propose and two others are physically attracted to her in the course of the narrative: there is never the slightest doubt that men will be after her. Hers is, to borrow a phrase of Mr Knightley's, the fate of thousands: it is not a fairy-story ending when a pretty and amusing girl marries well; it is life.

So though she uses Cinderella motifs, Jane Austen does not in the end follow the Cinderella story pattern. Furthermore, she seems keen not to encourage what one might call the Cinderella emotion: the gratification of fantasy through vicarious participation in a glamorous match. The plot imperatively requires Darcy to be rich and high-born. It is also conformable to the distinctive ethos of *Pride and Prejudice*—its peculiar light and sparkle—that its heroine, uniquely in these novels, should marry clearly above her sphere. But even in this case the hero is not given a title, though we might expect the owner of so grand and ancient an estate to be a baronet at the least. In similar spirit, our expectations of Mr Knightley's wealth are damped down; in the course of the narrative we learn, as it might seem casually, that he has little spare money and keeps no horses.[12] As we have seen, Jane Austen, the daughter of a country clergyman, had some high aristocrats among her kin; she had grander connections than any of her heroines.

There is a deliberate avoidance of trade in snob values. Nineteenth-century fiction is thick with lords and duchesses; the more striking, therefore, is Jane Austen's refusal to deal in that coin. *Cinderella*, like other pantomimes, ends with a wedding of glittering finery, all whiteness and spangles. The ending of *Emma* is, in this respect, an anti-Cinderella: the last word is left to Mrs Elton: 'Very little white satin, very few lace veils; a most pitiful business!' Recent film adaptations of Jane Austen contrast revealingly with the original. The BBC cast Belton House in the role of Rosings, with the result that Lady Catherine de Bourgh seemed if anything to under-estimate her own grandeur. In the film of *Emma* liveried footmen carrying stools attended Mr Knightley's guests in his garden. Such modern luxury-fantasies (sometimes imperfectly disguised as social criticism) betray the spirit of the books.[13]

Jane Austen tried to do only a few things; in the taxonomy of genius she belongs with Vermeer rather than Mozart. I do think that her unadventurousness (in one sense) came from a genuine awareness of her limits; I believe that she was sincere when she told the admirer who suggested some larger themes that if she took a clergyman for her principal character, she might be able to handle him from the side of comedy but not to represent his goodness and justice; and that she could no more write a historical romance than an epic poem. Yet it is easy to underestimate her range. It has been mischievously said of Bruckner that he did not write nine symphonies but the same symphony nine times; but one is not in the least tempted to say that Jane Austen wrote the same novel six times, any more than one would say that Vermeer kept painting the same picture (one might more justly say that of Monet, whose range is ostensibly wider). I want to stress her variety, within strict limits, because there are interpretations of her which flatten out this diversity and thus miss a large part of her art. We need not spend time on the idea of the novels as uniformly sweet-natured miniatures of village romance—that notion was laughed out of court many years ago. More scholarly, and more insidious, is the claim that the novels as a whole polemically advocate a particular moral, social, and political vision. *Emma*, as well as being an intense study of one individual woman, also seeks to depict a whole, small society. This book does suggest the importance of social duty and presents some idea of what constitutes a good society (though, as I shall argue, it does not advocate the cosy paternalism often attributed to it). The individual happiness of Emma and Knightley will also contribute to the well-being of their community; Knightley, the virtuous landowner devoted to the welfare of those around him, is indeed a pattern of the good gentleman, as lazy, selfish Mr Woodhouse is an example of the bad gentleman. But it is essential to understand that the study of the individual in relation to his or her community distinguishes *Emma* from the other works in the canon. Jane Austen is among the best of novelists at giving her readers the sense of a hinterland. In *Pride and Prejudice*, for example, though there is almost no description of place and the spotlight is upon the principal actors, we feel them to be planted in a solid and credible setting. That is important to the naturalism of the story. Darcy is a rich man, and a virtuous landlord; both these facts are required by the plot. But there is no sense that the union of Darcy and Elizabeth is, as the union of Emma and

Knightley will be, an act of social and communal importance. One school of criticism finds fault with *Pride and Prejudice* for not making more of the 'future life of active social involvement' which is supposedly adumbrated for Darcy and his wife.[14] This is misguided. It is an odd priggishness which decrees that novels ought to end with a moral and an injection of social responsibility. Jane Austen herself was indeed very funny on just this point, writing gaily to her sister Cassandra in a much quoted letter, 'The work is rather too light and bright and sparkling;—it wants shade;—it wants to be stretched out here and there with a long Chapter—of sense if it could be had, if not of solemn specious nonsense— about something unconnected with the story; an Essay on Writing, a critique on Walter Scott, or the history of Buonaparte—or anything that would form a contrast and bring the reader with increased delight to the playfulness and Epigrammatism of the general stile.—I doubt your quite agreeing with me here—I know your starched Notions.'[15]

Pride and Prejudice is a blithe comedy, and as such obeys its own laws of form and content. *Emma* explores new territory, because Jane Austen, within her self-imposed limits, is an ambitious writer, who wants to do different things. I shall argue that the author of *Mansfield Park* has not changed from the woman who wrote *Pride and Prejudice*: she has merely moved on to new ground. It is really not surprising that Shakespeare should write both *Hamlet* and *Twelfth Night*, or that a composer should create both a tragic and a comic symphony. Because Jane Austen's range is in some obvious respects so restricted, it becomes especially important to see that her range of tone and ethos is wide. In reality, the authorial persona is more various in her than in, say, George Eliot.

The distinctively exuberant comedy of *Pride and Prejudice* is at its most brilliant in the great showdown between Elizabeth and Lady Catherine in the garden at Longbourn. For many Janeites this is a favourite scene. But I know one shrewd reader who finds fault with it on the grounds that young Elizabeth could never in reality have been so self-possessed in such a situation or so sharp and resourceful in repartee. I do not know if other readers are likely to find force in this criticism, but I do think it worth while to take it seriously and consider what answer might be made. The exercise can tell us something about the peculiar art of this novel—both its theatricality and its method of handling a traditional story pattern.

In the first place, it looks as though Jane Austen was aware herself that this criticism might be made and took steps to meet it. In anticipation of this scene, Lizzy is made to answer back to Lady Catherine on her visit to Rosings, many chapters before, and Lady Catherine remarks on how forward she is for a young woman in expressing her own opinions. It is a datum of Lizzy's character that she is unusually bold, lively, quick-thinking, and self-possessed; and because she is so brilliantly realized, it is a datum that we can pretty readily accept. Moreover, Jane Austen does not allow Lizzy to win her battle with Lady Catherine hands down. ' "He is a gentleman; I am a gentleman's daughter; so far we are equal." '—Lizzy wins that one.[16] But Lady Catherine parries: ' "True. You *are* a gentleman's daughter. But who was your mother? Who are your uncles and aunts? . . ." ' That is a palpable hit, and effectively Elizabeth has no answer. Jane Austen's concern with naturalism allows Elizabeth to win only on points, not to triumph over-whelmingly. If we do find this episode not perfectly true to ordinary life, that goes to show how exceptionally high are the standards of naturalism that the reading of Jane Austen's novels has spoilt us into demanding. There is hardly another important novel, even among those written according to the canons of classic nineteenth-century realism, which does not contain scenes stretching the bounds of pure naturalism a good deal more than this. Perhaps because modernist and post-modern fiction has been in revolt against the realist tradition, we may underestimate how difficult a strong naturalism is to bring off convincingly.

No novel can be exactly true to life, if only because it would be too dull and redundant. But with Lady Catherine in the garden there is another consideration that we should bear in mind: the theatrical character of the scene. Many other books have a theatrical set-piece near the end: Agatha Christie, for example, quite often has Hercule Poirot gather the whole cast into the drawing room to tell them which of their number is the murderer. That is not in the least plausible, but it satisfies the senses of theatre and of closure. Of course Agatha Christie's books do not in any important sense resemble or interpret life, but the device can also be seen in a classic novel: at the end of *Martin Chuzzlewit* Dickens similarly arranges for most of the main characters to be gathered together in one place and dismissed, accord-ing to their deserts, to happiness or disgrace. This is pretty preposterous, but it does not matter, because Dickens has concerns other than simple realism: at this point at least the novel becomes pantomime and morality play. We enjoy the sense of grand finale, the stage crowded, the pleasures of partisanship and revenge gratified by seeing the good rewarded and the bad punished.

Jane Austen is of course far less florid than this, more covert, but she too has a sense of theatre at work. Elizabeth's scene with Lady Catherine is one among the series of duets which bring the novel to its denouement, but it is also a duel. It is consciously a great set-piece, like (say) the courtship duet between Millamant and Mirabell in *The Way of the World*. We revel in the virtuosity of Lizzy's resource and sharpness. As Lady Catherine gets her come-uppance we are right to see behind the modern brilliance the presence of an archetypal story pattern and to feel an atavistic pleasure. I suspect that Jane Austen is well enough aware that she is here stretching the bounds of purest naturalism a little bit. But it is only a very little bit, and with two happy consequences. One is that the reader is allowed a pure treat: the whole episode is, quite simply, enormous fun. The other is that great sophistication can be combined with a basic story pattern. It is wholly proper to the comedic spirit of *Pride and Prejudice* that the humble enjoyments of the fairy story or the folk tale should be felt and indulged for a little space—proper that we should both have the subtleties and equivocations of human nature anatomized, and get a chance to hiss the villain.

3

The Character of Character

Jane Austen slips into *Pride and Prejudice*, fairly early on, a discussion about the nature of character.[1] It is done with perfect ease—Elizabeth's talk with Bingley grows out of believable social banter and is then interrupted by Darcy and Mrs Bennet in the most natural way—but it is nevertheless, in the academic jargon, programmatic. Bingley perceives that Elizabeth is 'a studier of character'; she for her part maintains that some characters are 'deep and intricate', while others, like Bingley himself, are not. That is a statement about people themselves, not about how they are represented in fiction, and a novelist who thinks as Elizabeth does will present some major characters more simply than others not only for reasons of literary economy but also as part of a proper mimesis of the variety that exists in human nature. Darcy voices a complaint that has often been made about his creator's limitations: ' "The country," said Darcy, "can in general supply but few objects for such a study. In a country neighbourhood you move in a very confined and unvarying society."' But criticizing Jane Austen is among those faults of which Darcy needs to be cured. Elizabeth for her part replies that 'people themselves alter so much, that there is something new to be observed in them for ever'. There may be in this the idea that it takes time and experience to read some characters right; there is certainly the idea of character development. So three ideas seem to be presented by this passage: that some characters are by nature more complex than others; that characters may be difficult to assess correctly; and that character may alter. All three things, as it happens, will be observed in Darcy.

By 'character' Lizzy Bennet means the individual nature of real people, but literary critics also need to use the word 'character' to denote the representation of human beings in fiction. In these literary terms a distinction is often drawn between flat and rounded characters; it was given currency by E. M. Forster in his *Aspects of the Novel* (perhaps it is his own invention). The distinction seems a useful one; but Forster's book was made out of lectures, delivered in a pretty informal style, and upon a closer look it becomes harder to see quite what argument he is making. He acknowledges, of course, that the distinction is not absolute. The totally flat character, he says, is constructed 'round a single idea or quality; where there is more than one factor in them, we get the beginning of a curve toward the round'. The really flat character, he adds, can be expressed in one sentence, and he gives as an example Mrs Micawber, who can be expressed in the proposition, 'I will never desert Mr Micawber.' Not much later, however, Forster declares that almost all Dickens's people are flat, with the imperfect exceptions of David Copperfield and Pip. Why then does he choose as an example of flatness not (say) Mr Micawber but so very minor a figure as his wife? The truth is surely that Forster muddled together at least two different considerations. The significance of Mrs Micawber is that she is a background figure; we simply know very little about her. What differentiates her from her husband, or from Betsy Trotwood or Uriah Heep, is not that she is flatter than they but that she is more dimly lit. She is also (and this is yet another consideration) a dim personality, under her husband's shadow; that is a fact about her, not a style of presenting her. A dim personality could in principle be explored in a thoroughly 'rounded' way; indeed, there is hardly a better example of this in literature than Jane Austen's Fanny Price.

Dickens's masterpieces of character depiction are indeed flat, but in a quite different sense: far from being dim, they are very brightly painted, but on a two-dimensional surface. Pecksniff and Micawber and Mrs Gamp are wonderful studies of human behaviour, of speech and attitude, but it has been said that they have no insides: you could not imagine what it would be like to be Pecksniff or Mrs Gamp. And they must always act 'in character'—or at least, if they step out of character, it is likely to be unconvincing (Dickens tells us that Micawber becomes a respected magistrate in Australia, but notoriously no one has ever been able to believe him).

Let us take two cases where fictional people 'step out of character'. In the first case, the author is Dickens; the second case will bring us back to Jane Austen, and to Forster's comments upon her.

When Mr Bumble is delivering Oliver Twist into the hands of the undertaker Sowerberry, he is momentarily moved to compassion and has to hide his emotion, muttering something about his 'troublesome cough'.[2] Every reader feels that this is a false note, that Dickens is improperly tugging at our heartstrings. No one feels that a flat character has at this point acquired some roundness—that we are learning that the apparently callous and pompous Bumble is more complex, and has a sympathetic side. On the contrary, we think that Bumble is worse portrayed at this moment—that the pressure of sentimentality has distorted literary truthfulness.

Now let us turn to Jane Austen. Lady Bertram is, says Forster, a flat character; or rather, she is flat until the disaster of her daughter's adultery overtakes her:[3]

> Lady Bertram did not think deeply, but, guided by Sir Thomas, she thought justly on all important points; and she saw, therefore, in all its enormity, what had happened, and neither endeavoured herself, nor required Fanny to advise her, to think little of guilt and infamy.

Forster explains that he had once thought of this passage in the spirit with which I have suggested we think of Mr Bumble's queasy moment: he had reckoned that the character was pulled out of true by the author's moralism, as in *Oliver Twist* by the author's sentimentality. But Forster has changed his mind: Lady Bertram, he decides, is a flat character who here acquires some roundness, before subsiding into flatness once again.

As a piece of practical criticism Forster's analysis of this sentence may do well, but the terms in which he puts the issue are less happy. I do not myself think either that this sentence strikes a false note or that it develops Lady Bertram's character in a particularly interesting way (it does tell us something interesting and surprising about Fanny, but that is another matter, to which I shall return). It is more in the nature of a piece of tidying up; we need to know how she has reacted to Maria's disgrace, and in a few unemphatic sentences the author informs us. What we get is not something that enlarges our idea of Lady Bertram but something that confirms it. She is a very conventional woman, and a very passive one, who will take her opinions from her husband. When we hear how she reacts, our own response can be: Yes indeed, the circumstances are quite new, but that is exactly how Lady Bertram would feel. It misrepresents the case, therefore, to say that she has acquired a roundedness that she did not have before; rather, the passage confirms the solidity that has belonged to Jane Austen's conception of her all along.

Lady Bertram will indeed reward closer inspection. She seems the essence of the flat character or caricature, not because she is a comic grotesque, like Mrs Gamp or Lady Sneerwell, but because we seem to see her only in one mood and in one position, sunk in the bored torpor of joyless comfort on her sofa, with her pug beside her. But what will be the effect on her of the successive disasters which have struck her family? She has been absent from the book for many chapters at the point when Fanny returns to Mansfield Park from Portsmouth, and we may well be curious about how she will appear when we next see her. Jane Austen's answer is inspired.[4]

> Fanny had scarcely passed the solemn-looking servants when Lady Bertram came from the drawing room to meet her; came with no indolent step; and, falling on her neck, said, 'Dear Fanny!'

Is this the transformation through suffering, the redemption almost, of Lady Bertram? But I have left out the last five words of her address. Here it is in full:

'Dear Fanny! now I shall be comfortable.'

This is the sudden turn that the classical rhetoricians called *para prosdokian* (against expectation). The twist back into self-centredness is brilliantly managed, and with this quiet *coup de théâtre* Jane Austen closes her chapter.

But this is not just a comic or clever effect. It is a study of character. Lady Bertram has at least the possibility of changing, and indeed she has, to a degree, changed. 'Dear Fanny'—the affection is genuine, we do not doubt that, and the rush to greet Fanny is part of that affection, but Jane Austen studies the way in which friendship and self-gratification are intertwined. 'Comfortable' is the perfect word, so subtly and terribly different from 'comforted'. Lady Bertram can speak of human relations only in the terms in which one would assess the sofa where so much of her life is spent.

Lady Bertram is in Elizabeth Bennet's terms not an intricate character; she is easy to read. But it is Jane Austen's special art that the simple character can be an interesting psychological study. There is an interplay in Lady Bertram's lethargic mind between a mild fondness for other creatures and the business of making oneself cosy. Pug is not the same as the sofa, and Fanny is not the same as Pug, but all exist, for her, as ministrants to her faint gratifications. She is one of three sisters who through marriage have had widely different fates. Under other circumstances Lady Bertram could not have become like Mrs Norris—she lacks the gumption—but she might have become not unlike Mrs Price. Within Jane Austen's study of the psychopathology of boredom she represents one kind of outcome. She is not so much a flat character as a flattened character—her dull, pampered life has drained from her the possibility of variety of response. Or to put it another way, if there is flatness in her, that flatness is the point of her. The flatness is a truth about her nature rather than a description of the novelist's technique. Like the animal in the cartoon, she has been *squashed* flat.

We might think in terms of three dichotomies: between rounded and flat characters, between complex and simple characters, and between described and undescribed (or developed and undeveloped) characters. These pairs overlap, but they are not the same. Jane Austen is unusually good at giving the sense of a hinterland, which signifies even if has not been visited. For one of the most delicate aspects of her craft is her ability to suggest, even with minor characters, that there is more to them than we see, or that they can be interpreted in more than one way. Most novelists offer the impression, whether with the minor or major players in their drama, that they have given us all of the character that there is to be had; many novelists, indeed, tend to tell us too much about minor characters, as though sheer quantity of information were a way of turning two dimensions into three. (It would be easy enough to illustrate this from respected writers of the present day.) Jane Austen understands the virtue in making gradations between background and foreground. This feeling is partly aesthetic: a sense of literary economy, of focusing on the action and the people that really count, a discipline that refuses to be distracted by 'too many details of right hand and of left'. But it also represents the greater truth to life: in the case of people we know casually, in their social setting, there will always be much that is unseen, and their characters may be open to a variety of interpretation. A sense of the hidden, the implicit, or the uncertain provides more real depth and solidity than a host of minor players all lit with the same brightness and kitted out with a set of explicit characteristics.

John Knightley notes that Mr Elton can be 'rational and unaffected' when he is with men: it is among women that he strains affectedly to be agreeable. The other Knightley, who has had more opportunity to observe Elton, has already noticed that in unreserved moments, 'when there are only men present', his sentimental language fades and his talk permits the deduction that he means to marry money.[5] Of course we ourselves never see Mr Elton when there are only men present, but the judgements of both brothers carry immediate credibility. They also add some small complexity: we realize that we have seen neither the worst of Elton nor the best of him.

Some characters, as Elizabeth Bennet says, are simple by nature. 'She is pretty,' Mr Knightley remarks of Harriet Smith, 'and she is good tempered, and that is all.' Near the end of the book he will say that he has developed his view of her: he now recognizes her good qualities, and is convinced that she is 'an artless, amiable girl' with 'seriously good principles', who places her happiness in the pleasures of domestic life.[6] But perhaps this claim to an adjustment of opinion is mainly a courtesy to Emma, and in any case it hardly develops his idea of Harriet much. Essentially, she is represented as very nearly flat because she is very nearly flat.

Mr Weston, a much more minor figure, who may seem at least as simply drawn, is interestingly different. He may appear to be merely a shrewder version of Sir William Lucas, and each may appear to be no more than one of the Cheeryble brothers. But Jane Austen's treatment of them illustrates how she differs from Dickens in the representation of minor characters. Even Sir William—certainly a simple, not an intricate character, in Lizzy Bennet's terms—has a small degree of roundedness: he may be an amiable old buffer, but he is also too pleased with himself. Mr Weston is a subtler study. His warmth and energy delight us, but John Knightley takes a cooler view, telling his wife that Mr Weston must not have too much minded handing over his son to adoption:[7]

> But you need not imagine Mr. Weston to have felt what you would feel in giving up Henry or John. Mr. Weston is rather an easy, cheerful tempered man, than a man of strong feelings; he takes things as he finds them, and makes enjoyment of them somehow or other, depending, I suspect, much more upon what is called *society* for his comforts, that is, upon the power of eating and drinking, and playing whist with his neighbours five times a-week, than upon family affection, or any thing that home affords.

Few novelists would have bothered to round out a background character in this way, fewer still to attribute a deficiency in the finer and deeper emotions to a background character who is obviously designed—and successfully designed—to be lovable. John Knightley turns out to be right: some fifty pages on, when Frank Churchill proves unable to come to Highbury after all, Mrs Weston is more upset at missing the stepson whom she has never seen than her husband is about his own flesh and blood.[8]

Novels are likely to include people who play only a minimal part in the action, and even some who remain off-stage, so to speak, appearing only in the conversation of others. Such figures are characters in the story, in a sense, but it does not seem appropriate to speak of them as having character. But Jane Austen at her best has the power to give them another quality—what one might call substance. Miss Nash in *Emma*, for instance, who barely exists for us outside the utterances of Harriet Smith, manages to be intensely present to the imagination, though absent from the action. Sometimes, indeed, a novelist will not want to engage the reader's imagination; there are moments when briskness is best. Here, for example, is a sentence from *Emma* that any novelist might have written:[9]

> The marriage of Lieut. Fairfax, of the —— regiment of infantry, and Miss Jane Bates, had had its day of fame and pleasure, hope and interest; but nothing now remained of it, save the melancholy remembrance of him dying in action abroad—of his widow sinking under consumption and grief soon afterwards—and this girl.

Jane Austen is simply dispatching a bit of business here—explaining Jane Fairfax's background. We are not involved in her parents' story, and are not meant to be. The tragical history of Fairfax and his Jane would be another book. But here by contrast is another off-stage event vastly slighter, yet far more significant. It is part of a rhapsody by Harriet over Mr Elton:[10]

> And so excellent in the Church! Miss Nash has put down all the texts he has ever preached from since he came to Highbury. Dear me! When I look back to the first time I saw him! How little did I think!—The two Abbotts and I ran into

the front room and peeped through the blind when we heard he was going by, and Miss Nash came and scolded us away, and staid to look through herself; however, she called me back presently, and let me look too, which was very good-natured. And how beautiful we thought he looked! He was arm in arm with Mr. Cole.

A effusion such as this is perhaps as near as Jane Austen ever gets to a capacity of which Dickens, along with Shakespeare, is the supreme master—the power to imbue the full flow of everyday, foolish, or uneducated speech with an odd poetry. Ordinarily, she is among the least poetic of novelists, whether in her own voice or in the utterances of her characters. Miss Bates and Flora Finching are two of literature's greatest babblers, but the surreal romance and beautiful absurdity of, say, Flora's picture of Little Dorrit in Italy are quite outside Jane Austen's range. Yet in Harriet's effusion there is a special kind of art. The twentieth century has been fascinated by the 'unreliable narrator', in many kinds of fiction, from *Doktor Faustus* and *The Good Soldier* to Bertie Wooster, but it is a hard trick to bring off. If your narrator is meant to be pompous, dull-witted, or immoral, how can he be skilled at story-telling or the vehicle for conveying subtle perceptions? Well, Jane Austen can do it. For a few sentences Harriet is an 'unreliable narrator'. Her chatter is an entirely naturalistic representation of a simple girl's artless gush, yet at the same time it has a touch of poignancy. And the narrative has an unexpected density: a whole scene is developed in one sentence—the rush of the girls to the window, then their retreat, then Miss Nash's change of mind (why?—because she does not want to betray herself too far, or because she hungers to have fellow-worshippers join her in the cult of

Mr Elton?). Last, we catch the momentary, minimal envy of Mr Cole, who can possess the felicity of Mr Elton's arm.

'And staid to look through herself'—there can be hardly a figure in fiction who has a slighter presence on the page than Miss Nash, and yet though she remains off-stage, she is fully substantial in this tiny glimpse of vain longing. We shall never meet her, but we shall get one further glimpse of her feelings, even briefer and more indirect. Passing Mr Elton's vicarage with Emma, Harriet exclaims, 'Oh!—what a sweet house!—How very beautiful! There are the yellow curtains that Miss Nash admires so much.'[11] Mr Elton will not readily have invited Miss Nash into his home: she may not have seen much more of the curtains than their lining. Here we find also that feeling for the significance of objects which first emerges in *Mansfield Park*: the yellow curtains belong with the green baize looted by Mrs Norris, the stump of Mr Elton's pencil, and Betsey's knife, simple bits of substance infused with the music of humanity.

The flat character, in Forster's sense, cannot surprise us. When Bumble shows a touch of humanity, we do not believe it; for Uriah Heep to do an unselfish deed would be absurd. Mary Bennet is flat in that way: if she were to stop being a sententious prig, she would cease to exist at all. But that is remarkably rare in Jane Austen. We can apply this test to fictional people: given a new situation, can we predict how they will react? Can they, while remaining in character, leave us uncertain how they will behave? Some of Jane Austen's characters, too easily labelled caricatures, can in fact keep us guessing. Mrs Norris and her sister are a case in point. These may seem to be invariable characters: Lady Bertram is always luxurious and indolent; and Mrs Norris is unvarying at least in her bitterness and malice. But when Fanny refuses Henry Crawford's proposal of marriage they face an unexpected turn of events: how will they now feel? As a spokesman for dutiful obedience, Mrs Norris is of course bitterly angry with Fanny for turning Henry down, but there is a complication, for malice is a stronger emotion still: 'she was more angry with Fanny for having received such an offer, than for refusing it.'[12] As a piece of psychological observation, that seems absolutely truthful. Lady Bertram, on the other hand, who lives only in the present, with no sense of consequences, and who sees only surface, is gratified: she had been a beauty all her life, and had married well, and the fact that a man of fortune wants Fanny and thinks her pretty convinces Lady Bertram that she is pretty, and 'made her feel a sort of credit in calling her niece'.

I doubt whether we have been expecting this reaction: we would rather expect this most conventional woman to take the conventional view, asserted by her husband and her sister, that the poor relation is foolish and ungrateful to turn down the rich suitor. But once we hear what Lady Bertram feels, we should recognize, I believe, that this is exactly how she would feel. We might recall the author's observation, much earlier in the book, that Lady Bertram 'felt all the injuries of beauty in Mrs. Grant's being so well settled in life without being handsome'.[13] Her self-centredness, her treatment of Fanny as a superior kind of pet, whom it would be satisfying for others to admire, and her failure to see anything beyond external appearance lead her into an attitude that might not have been predicted, but once revealed, seems inevitable. It is a fine and bitter irony that the thoughtful Sir

Thomas should be so much more wrong than his empty-headed wife: he can purpose to do Fanny so much more harm for the very reason that, in his misguided way, he cares for her interests.

Even Mrs Bennet is not wholly predictable. When Elizabeth finally accepts Mr Darcy, we wait to find out what her mother's reaction will be. Will Mrs Bennet's apparently rooted and intense dislike of the man prove unalterable, or will she be overjoyed by the fact that her daughter has made so rich a catch? It is not only we who are unsure of the answer: Elizabeth herself, who knows her a great deal better than we do, is uncertain—that is a very fine touch. Once we know the answer—that Mrs Bennet is thrilled without a moment's hesitation—most readers, I suspect, say to themselves, 'Yes, of course—really I never doubted it for a moment.' But that too is a success on the author's part.[14]

In classical antiquity there was more than one theory about the character of character, but the predominant view was that each person was born with a particular moral disposition—in Greek, *ethos*. Circumstances might restrict the expression of that *ethos* or they might allow it full play, but essentially it was innate. Thus the historian Tacitus presents the emperor Tiberius as a bad man from the start. His behaviour, however, changed and developed throughout his life, as the people who had restrained his natural tendencies died off one by one and the true Tiberius emerged. Yet Tacitus does allow one of the people in his narrative to present what looks like a different view, arguing that Tiberius was disturbed and changed by the effect of exercising supreme power; this is similar to Acton's famous maxim that all power tends to corrupt and absolute power tends to corrupt absolutely. In reading modern biographies, and even more autobiographies, we can often feel that the accounts of childhood are the best part; sometimes it can seem that only the last sixty years are a bit disappointing. This is because we, for our own part, cherish a sense that character is itself malleable, not fully determined at birth but capable of alteration, especially in the early part of life. But in ancient biographies, the few anecdotes of childhood are never illuminating, for they represent the child merely as a pocket-sized version of the adult that he will become, displaying in infancy the *ethos* that he will display in manhood: little Cato playing at making laws and sending people to prison, little Cyrus playing at being a king, or—in the only story of Christ's boyhood preserved in the gospels—the young Jesus in the temple confuting the scribes and doctors of the law.

But if we do not, in life, fully subscribe to the *ethos* theory, our fiction on the whole does. This is obviously true of a creator of caricatures and grotesques like Dickens (though in his first-person novels, *David Copperfield* and *Great Expectations*, he does produce, by contrast, two of the finest depictions of character formation in childhood and adolescence ever written). It makes no sense to ask what made Pecksniff into a hypocrite; to pose the question is to misunderstand the rules of the game that Dickens is playing. Less obviously, I think that the same principle may also apply pretty much to novelists renowned for psychological complexity. Consider the people in Proust or Henry James, for example: they may change in mood or understanding, they may learn hard lessons, but I doubt whether we often see them change their inner nature much. Jane Austen is perhaps unusual in the extent to which she shows the moulding of character, for good or bad.

This is a subtle and difficult topic. In reality the distinction between the idea of an innate *ethos* and the idea of character being shapable by circumstance, or by moral effort, is not as clear cut as I have represented it. Change of behaviour, if it is permanent, is barely if at all to be distinguished from change of nature. Mary Crawford is sure that if her brother had succeeded in marrying Fanny, he would have become quite different: 'She would have fixed him.'[15] Does this mean that he would have changed into a virtuous man, or that his bad tendencies would have been kept in check? Since we cannot see into men's souls, we might instead ask what difference there is, outwardly, between these two things. What indeed is virtue? Is it the will to resist strong temptation or the development of a character which is above such temptation? What matters is that Jane Austen's people have enough solidity for such ambiguity as exists in life to remain in her fiction. We see the corruption of Mr Elton as the consequence of his marriage, shown in the unkindness of his open scorning of Harriet.[16] He is naturally a vain, weak man, but Mrs Elton is making him worse. Is his character being changed or his true nature coming out? We do not need to decide: it is enough to recognize the psychological truth.

In several places Jane Austen says explicitly that character is mutable and capable of being formed, especially in youth. She recognizes the significance of both nature and nurture. Mr Knightley's view is that Emma's character is a mixture of both: 'Nature gave you understanding:—Miss Taylor gave you principles. You must have done well.'[17] That agrees with what the author has said herself in the opening chapter, where, however, she also indicates that Miss Taylor was not firm enough to shape Emma as much as would have been best for her. It is a recurrent theme in these novels that women shape their husbands' characters, at least in terms of outward behaviour. The idea that husbands form their wives is also present, though less conspicuously. And the experience of married life is itself formative. Mrs Price and Mrs Norris would have been different if they had married differently (in the latter case this is explicit). With a more rational wife, we may suspect, Mr Bennet might not have been so private and reclusive in his pleasures.

D. W. Harding said that Jane Austen's people can be divided into characters and caricatures, and I expect that a good many readers agree with him.[18] In some limited sense his claim is no doubt true; but the argument I want to make is that this division is unhelpful, and that in important ways it distorts the nature of Jane Austen's art. Harding explains that some of her figures 'are offered as full and natural portraits of imaginable people; others while certainly referring to types of people we might easily have come across are yet presented with such exaggeration and simplification that our response to them is expected to be rather different'. Actually, that is truer of Scott, Dickens, Thackeray, George Eliot (of Fanny Burney and Maria Edgeworth, for that matter) than of Jane Austen—truer, in short, of almost any English novelist before the later nineteenth century. We would do better to see her as a novelist in whom the usual division between naturalistic portrayal and caricature virtually breaks down.

As a first observation, we might note that there is a difficulty in knowing what is and what is not realistic in the satirical depiction of a society remote from our own. Are Juvenal's depictions of Roman decadence, for example, meant to be read as baroque exaggerations, or was life like that? The experience of modern middle-class life does not give one much help in answering that kind of question. Sometimes Jane Austen can seem to be almost our contemporary, but her society was of course profoundly unlike today's: it was a different organism, with a different pathology. As it happens, I did myself once know a rich, aristocratic lady, a mixture of autocratic contempt and loneliness, who was more like Lady Catherine de Bourgh than one might otherwise have thought possible: tax and the death of deference may now have done for the type, but once it may not have been uncommon. Similarly, the peculiar blend of self-assertion and abasement in Mr Collins exhibits the psychopathology of a society stratified in terms of class. Of course he is a joke; but students of social history might find him worth their attention too.

Harding illustrates his distinction between caricatures and characters with a series of contrasted pairs from five of the novels: Mr Collins and Wickham, Mrs Jennings and Lucy Steele, Mrs Elton and Harriet Smith, Mrs Norris and Mrs Grant, Sir Walter Elliot and Mr Elliot. But the real distinctions here are other: between older and younger, the noisy and the restrained, the garrulous and the self-contained, or the colourful and the cool. I do not see, for example, that Mrs Jennings is any less of a character than Lucy Steele; but her manner is undoubtedly more broad and extrovert. Miss Bates is ripely comical, but she is also, at moments, poignant, and one might wonder whether a caricature can be quite that. No great harm is done by calling people like Mr Collins and Mrs Elton caricatures (I have already agreed that this is in a limited sense true); the real damage comes when a profound study like Mrs Norris is given that label. That is to confuse caricature with strength or vividness of personality.

And after all, absurd people do exist in real life, and other people recognize their absurdity. That is how Mr Collins is treated in *Pride and Prejudice*: from the first Mr Bennet regards him as preposterous, an object of comedy. That is a hazardous thing for a novelist to do—the author risks drawing attention to the artificiality of his creation, or the reader may not agree that the character is funny—and it is worth asking why Jane Austen succeeds. For the trick to come off it is necessary, paradoxically, for Mr Collins not to be entirely a flat character. Imagine someone in *The Importance of Being Earnest* pointing out that Lady Bracknell or Miss Prism is a caricature; that would bring the whole house of cards down. Mr Bennet can treat Mr Collins as an object of mockery because he is, in fact, something more than an object— because both men are solid figures in a naturalistic novel.

Naturalism in literature is mostly a matter of surfaces: the dialogue should be convincing, the plot believable, the characters not exaggerated beyond what might be met with in real life. Through history, most fiction has not been naturalistic: the *Iliad* and the *Aeneid* are not naturalistic, because people do not fight with gods or talk in verse; *The Golden Ass* is not naturalistic, because people do not turn into donkeys; Rabelais, Cervantes, and Swift are not naturalistic, for reasons too obvious to spell out. And this has been because much of what we value in the literary representation of men and women is not the surface but the sense of three-dimensionality, of psychological penetration and truth. We can illustrate the distinction from a less pretending genre than the literary novel—the television sitcom. Most sitcoms are fantastically unlike real life, particularly perhaps those that most overtly claim to be presenting a lifelike portrayal of ordinary people. *Fawlty Towers*, on the other hand, which I take to be one of the most substantial works of art created in the last thirty years, contains some obviously farcical elements (starting with the title); yet it is far more truthful than most sitcoms—and indeed, in many ways, more naturalistic too. Take the setting, for example. The sets of most sitcoms look like the stage sets that they are, but the interiors of Fawlty Towers were so beautifully observed that it was hard to believe the shows were not shot on location. Mr and Mrs Fawlty themselves were grotesques, but they were, so to speak, real grotesques. Their emotions were credibly motivated, and you could believe that they had a history: one could understand how this difficult, sardonic man and this once pretty, irredeemably vulgar woman could have managed to get themselves married to one another. Indeed, the Fawltys are probably nearer to Mr and Mrs Bennet than anyone else in recent fiction. One might add that the show was pitch perfect: had either of the Fawltys been only a little bit more sympathetic, they might have been almost tragic, but the comic discipline was always preserved—there is a touch of the Austen spirit in that too.

Jane Austen's novels aim both at strong naturalism and at psychological penetration: they are a pretty close mimesis of real life in its external manifestations and they also try to dig deep. We talk about characters in books being solid or three-dimensional, and most of her people fit that metaphor, more or less, but commonly she can give the sense that they have existed in a fourth dimension also, that of time. This can be true even of her comic figures: they not only exist, but they have come from somewhere. I concede that Mary Bennet is indeed a caricature, more crudely drawn than anything else in *Pride and Prejudice* (I suspect that Jane Austen permitted her survival because it allowed Mr Bennet to play off her with such brilliant unkindness), but even she has a reason for her priggish sententiousness: it is how the plain daughter finds a way of asserting herself among her pretty sisters.

Mr Collins for his part, though broadly and obviously ridiculous, is at the same time a subtler study than has often been realized. It is interesting to see how later interpreters have caricatured him in ways that his creator avoided. Thus in Charles E. Brock's charming late-Victorian illustrations he is depicted as a lank stringy fellow, apparently in his forties at least, with beaky features and a sanctimonious leer. In the BBC series he was played as Uriah Heep. This is mere inattention, not the consequence of any failure on Jane Austen's part to represent him clearly. Mr Collins is in fact 'a tall, heavy looking man of five and twenty'.[19] (There seems to be a common reluctance among readers to believe that people can be both large and young: Robert Louis Stevenson explicitly describes Long John Silver as big, pale, and amiable, with a face the size of a ham, but films and illustrations never represent him so.) He is not entirely simple, but a compound. Clever Mr Bennet spots this even before meeting him, merely from reading his letter: it contains 'a mixture of servility and self-importance . . ., which promises well'. A few pages later the same compound judgement is repeated in the author's own voice: he is 'altogether a mixture of pride and obsequiousness, self-importance and humility'. He too has come from somewhere, and his adult character has derived from a blend of nature and nurture: 'Mr. Collins was not a sensible man, and the deficiency of nature had been but little assisted by education or society.'[20] The analysis that follows develops a fair amount of complexity: a crushing father had given him humility of manner, later counteracted by 'the self-conceit of a weak head', the experience of living in retirement, and the effect of sudden and unexpected prosperity. Even his incumbency works doubly upon him, his consciousness of his position producing both a sense of his parsonical authority and a veneration of his patroness. Faced with Mr Collins's personality, one can intelligibly ask the questions 'why?' and 'how?' It would make no sense to ask them about Mrs Gamp or Skimpole or Micawber.

Mr Collins's proposal is of course a classic of farce. But compare it with a couple of other proposals written by two other famously funny authors, and it appears rather different. This is Oscar Wilde's Algernon, in *The Importance of Being Earnest*:

> Miss Cardew, ever since half-past twelve this afternoon, when I first looked upon your wonderful and incomparable beauty, I have not merely been your abject slave and servant, but, soaring upon the pinions of a possibly monstrous ambition, I have dared to love you wildly, passionately, devotedly, hopelessly . . . It is the beginning of an entirely new existence for me, and it shall be followed by such notes of admiration that my whole life shall be a subtle and sustained symphony of Love, Praise and Adoration combined.

And here is P. G. Wodehouse's George Mulliner:[21]

> It cannot have escaped your notice that I have long enter-

tained towards you sentiments warmer and deeper than those of ordinary friendship. It is love, Susan, that has been animating my bosom. Love, first a tiny seed, has burgeoned in my heart till, blazing into flame, it has swept away on the crest of its wave my diffidence, my doubt, my fears, and my foreboding, and now, like the topmost topaz of some ancient tower, it cries to all the world in a voice of thunder: 'You are mine! My mate! . . .' [—and so on].

Mr Collins's overture is, in its style and content, pretty similar to George Mulliner's: 'You can hardly doubt the purpose of my discourse, however your natural delicacy may lead you to dissemble; my attentions have been too marked to be mistaken.' Yet there is a huge difference in the literary effect. The proposals in Wilde and Wodehouse are purely absurd: we do not believe, and are not meant to believe, that any real suitor would speak like that. But Mr Collins's is an absurdity plausibly formed by his individual character. No one is more unpopular than the person who insists on explaining the jokes, and so I shrink from a detailed discussion of Mr Collins's address, but as a study of character it does repay a close analysis, clause by clause. I will content myself with just one: 'And now nothing remains for me but to assure you in the most animated language of the violence of my affection.' There may be no funnier sentence in English fiction than this, but one can observe, at the risk of portentousness, that it represents a distinctive character and experience: the habit of sermonizing and arranging one's discourse under heads; the speaker's half-understanding of worldly behaviour and of the language of romance (soon to be further displayed in his deluded ideas about the 'usual practice of elegant females').[22] Dickens's grotesques tend to be monologuists, who stand apart from the action of the story; Mr Collins too aspires to the condition of monologue, but in his case because it is his character to be unaware of his effect on anyone else. His solipsism becomes part of the story, one of the minor mechanisms which drive the action forward.

Some novelists are more skilful at creating characters (or caricatures) than at connecting them one with another. But Jane Austen is practised in the art of connection: she can paint the conversation piece as well as the portrait. Much of this deftness is unobtrusive, developed in casual scenes, of no great importance. *Pride and Prejudice* will offer us an example.[23] The setting is Rosings, Lady Catherine's house in Kent, with Lizzy seated at the piano; she has started to encourage Colonel Fitzwilliam to join her in teasing Darcy. (Three people in dialogue, we might note in passing, are harder to handle well than a conversation between two.) Elizabeth declares that she is about to reveal something 'very dreadful' about Darcy's conduct in Hertfordshire: he attended a ball -

'... and at this ball, what do you think he did? He danced only four dances! I am sorry to pain you—but so it was. He danced only four dances, though gentlemen were scarce; and, to my certain knowledge, more than one young lady was sitting down in want of a partner. Mr Darcy, you cannot deny the fact.'

'I had not at that time the honour of knowing any lady in the assembly beyond my own party.'

'True; and nobody can ever be introduced in a ball room. Well, Colonel Fitzwilliam, what do I play next? My fingers wait your orders.'

'Perhaps,' said Darcy, 'I should have judged better, had I

sought an introduction, but I am ill qualified to recommend myself to strangers.'

This is of course one small episode in the battle of wits and passions between Elizabeth and Darcy, and the words which most novelists would not have included, or would have placed a little later, are, 'Well, Colonel Fitzwilliam, what do I play next? My fingers wait your orders.' Their placing here indicates that Darcy *interrupts*. Lizzy has made her little sally and closed the conversation. She has gone back to her music, and since it is a convention that gentlemen are always longing for the delight of hearing a lady play, it is very slightly impolite of Darcy to prevent her. What has happened? Darcy has not had the quickness of mind to reply on the instant, but he does not want to let the matter lie: he feels the need, half to apologize, half to defend himself. The passage unfolds, like a scene on stage, as pure dialogue, almost without authorial guidance or explanation (for this is yet another instance of theatrical method in *Pride and Prejudice*). In less deft an author it might have gone like this:

> 'True; and nobody can ever be introduced in a ball room.'
> Satisfied with this small triumph and anxious to leave Mr
> Darcy no opportunity to reply, she turned back to his cousin
> and continued at once, 'Well, Colonel Fitzwilliam what do I
> play next? My fingers wait your orders.' But before he in
> turn could answer, Darcy broke in. 'Perhaps I should have
> judged better . . .'

But Jane Austen has done all this without any stage directions whatever. The moment passes so swiftly and easily that it may seem ponderous to dwell upon it, but the craft is subtle and very fine. This little passage contributes, in its small way, to the action of the story: it reveals that Darcy now cares (as on his first appearance in the book he did not) what somebody in Hertfordshire thinks about him: we witness his emotions becoming engaged with Elizabeth. And it contributes to the book's—and its heroine's—enquiry into Darcy's nature. Is this pride or the abating of pride? Pride, Mary has obligingly told us a hundred pages before, is different from vanity; 'Pride relates more to our opinion of ourselves, vanity to what we would have others think of us.'[24] The company go on to discuss Darcy's character. Asked by Elizabeth why Darcy should be, as he claims to be, ill qualified to recommend himself to strangers, Fitzwilliam answers that it is because Darcy will not give himself the trouble. Darcy, for his part, attributes it to a deficiency of social talent. Earlier in the book his statements about himself were enigmatic: we might doubt whether he was admitting to some weakness or praising himself with faint damns. Was he, in fact, congratulating himself on his integrity in the very act of apparent self-criticism? Now, at Rosings, we may suspect a slight shift to something more genuinely self-deprecating.

One of the ways by which Jane Austen connects her characters is through the representation of family likeness. In bad fiction (and in some good fiction) the members of a family may seem to have nothing in common: the hero has a wicked brother, the evil father has a saintly daughter, and heaven alone knows why. Bingley is quite unlike his sisters, and Anne Elliot quite unlike the rest of her family (except, we are told, her dead mother), but one has only to cite such cases to realize that in Jane Austen they are comparatively uncommon. In *Pride and Prejudice* the facts of kinship are presented in a fairly straightforward way: Lydia Bennet is very plainly her mother's child, and Elizabeth her father's (and each is the favourite of the respective parent). But Elizabeth's heredity, like her character, is more complex than Lydia's, for her nature is the product of both her parents: though her intelligence and humour come from her father, she displays them through characteristics that are not at all his: her liveliness and extroversion and even the way she pushes her talk to the limits of social propriety evidently come from her mother. She is more like the mother she despises than she knows; the smoothness of Jane Austen's craftsmanship may disguise how clever that is.

In *Mansfield Park* we recognize a kinship of character, as of blood, between Henry and Mary Crawford: the selfishness and worldliness, the wit and sparkle, the pleasure in performance and the urge to conquer, yet combined with moral taste. I shall come back to them later. But it is perhaps in *Emma* above all that kinship is explored. With simpler characters the kinship is, appropriately, more simply depicted. Neither Mr Weston nor his son Frank Churchill is an intricate character, but both have a liveliness which shades into restlessness—both must always be doing and moving. This trait is more overt in Frank, as befits a younger man. He first reaches Highbury a day before he is expected.[25] His father understands why: the impatience, the energy, the pleasure in taking one's friends by surprise: 'I told you all that he would be here before the time named.' But Mr Weston had predicted that Frank would come an hour before his time, whereas Frank is actually early by some twenty hours.

The quick, severe sharpness of Mr Knightley is seen

again, in more acid and censorious style, in his younger brother. John Knightley is more cynical and more entertaining, impatient but acute. But he shares the elder brother's tendency to lecture Emma:[26]

> 'Mr. Elton in love with me!—What an idea!'
> 'I do not say that it is so; but you will do well to consider whether it is so or not, and to regulate your behaviour accordingly. I think your manners to him encouraging. I speak as a friend, Emma. You had better look about you, and ascertain what you do, and what you mean to do.'

This sounds very like the elder Knightley, but it is a touch more rapid and abrupt (except for the famous scene in which Mr Knightley rebukes Emma for her rudeness to Miss Bates, but that is, significantly, a special case). The comparison helps to define the elder Knightley: the fact that he is so like his brother, though more gracious in manner, brings out his tendency to swift, hard judgement, and a kind of anger in him, but also shows how well disciplined his emotions are for the most part.

Emma herself is not entirely unlike her father: they share a lack of ambition and a contentment with being important within a very small sphere. That is what keeps her attached to Mr Woodhouse: Elizabeth Bennet would have got away from him, and Fanny Price would have despised him. But we are told at the outset that he could be 'no companion' to Emma; she gets her intelligence from her long dead mother. Her sister Isabella, on the other hand, inherits his amiable silliness. We see this, for example, in the broadly comic scene in which the two wrangle about illnesses and treatments, each backing their own physician: Perry says this, and Mr Wingfield says that.[27] In later life, we reflect, Mrs John

Knightley is likely to become as much a valetudinarian as her parent. Much more subtle is a likeness unobtrusively suggested in two widely separated scenes. Early in the story, Mr Woodhouse breaks into a discussion between Emma and Knightley: ' "Emma never thinks of herself, if she can do good to others;" rejoined Mr. Woodhouse, understanding but in part.' Ten chapters on, Isabella breaks into a conversation between her husband and father: ' "Me, my love," cried his wife, hearing and understanding only in part.'[28] Father and daughter share the same placid, lazy spirits, drifting in and out of the talk but neither sharp nor curious enough to grasp the whole of it.

The strangest and most moving kinship revealed in *Emma*, however, is between two people who are neither blood relations nor lovers. It is a mark of Jane Austen's daring and truthfulness that she can represent the heroes and heroines as less like one another than they are like other characters in the story. In *Emma*, accordingly, the ecstasy duet is not between Emma and Knightley but between her and Frank Churchill, as they celebrate each their own felicity and extol their future spouses. (I am reminded of the great duet about the heavenliness of married love in *The Magic Flute*, not between Pamina and Tamino but between Pamina and Papageno, so that the idea of the holiness of love extends to the comic couple as well as the serious pair, embracing both the prince and the birdcatcher.) Emma recognizes that there must have been a part of Frank that enjoyed the deception he was practising; and she recognizes it because she would have enjoyed it herself. They share a sense of mischief and fun. They enjoy recalling the awkwardnesses of the past, as Frank's bride does not: 'How you can bear such

recollections, [says Jane Fairfax] is astonishing to me!—
They *will* sometimes obtrude—but how you can *court*
them!'²⁹ Frank has wanted to have the pleasure of teasing
Jane, but we can see that this is a pleasure which he will never
have from his wife (just as Mr Knightley will not manage to
get Emma to call him George). There is an absolute honesty
about this—a recognition that even in the best marriage
there is not a perfect match of temperament and style. At the
same time, Jane Austen's imagination reveals a maturity and
range which is able to encompass different kinds of relationship—which sees that sexual love does not exclude other
kinds of closeness and empathy. The fact that Emma can
share a certain kind of spirit more readily with Frank than
with Knightley does not make us doubt the rightness of
Emma's marriage. As for Frank and Jane—the pair who
despite her quiet seriousness are the Papageno and
Papagena of this story, because they do not go so deep, or in
Lizzy Bennet's terms are not intricate characters—we may
perhaps agree with Mr Knightley: given her goodness of
nature, he has a fair chance of doing well. But if the marriage
succeeds (and that is left less than fully certain), it will be
through the complementarity of difference.

In *Pride and Prejudice* Elizabeth is both like and unlike her
father, both like and unlike Mr Darcy. It is worth tracing
how the word 'absurd' behaves in this novel. In Mr Bennet's
mouth it is linked to the human comedy. Mr Collins's belief
that Elizabeth will soon be engaged to Darcy is 'delightfully
absurd'. Is there a risk that Lydia Bennet's wild manner may
put off some of her sisters' lovers?—'Such squeamish youths
as cannot bear to be connected with a little absurdity, are not
worth a regret.'³⁰ Lizzy shares her father's sense of the

comic, but with a harsher edge, and when she uses the word 'absurd', it is in bitter reproach against herself: ashamed of falling for Wickham's story about Darcy and himself, she feels that she has been 'blind, partial, prejudiced, absurd'. Darcy's letter briskly excuses the offensive things that he will say about Elizabeth's family: 'The necessity must be obeyed—and farther apology would be absurd.' Later he will confess to Bingley the occurrences that have made his former interference in Bingley's affairs 'impertinent and absurd'.[31] For all their differences, Elizabeth and Darcy share a tart idea of the human scene, with an edge of scorn (Darcy accuses himself of having wished to think meanly of people, and Elizabeth is described, for example, as enjoying her dislike of Bingley's sisters);[32] and both have an angry pride that feels error as humiliation. It is telling that they should each turn the word 'absurd' against themselves in indignant self-contempt.

Jane Austen exhibits in *Pride and Prejudice* the rare gift of being able to represent different senses of humour. Even in very fine humorists, like Wilde, Saki, or Wodehouse, one usually finds that all the characters, or at least all those capable of amusing talk, share the same comic style and idiolect. Jane Austen, however, presents an interplay of kinship and difference. Doubtless, Elizabeth gets her wit and intelligence from her father; yet her sense of humour is not the same. He characteristically sports with incongruity, linguistic or otherwise. 'I must trouble you once more for congratulations.' 'Trouble' is of course the ironic word: we would expect either 'I must trouble you for'—the return of a loan, or whatever; or 'You will be delighted to hear the good news that . . .' 'While Mary is adjusting her ideas'—but of course you do not adjust ideas to order: you either have them or you do not. 'You have delighted us long enough'—we expect either 'You have gone on long enough' or 'That was delightful'.[33] Mr Bennet's wit, most often based on a play with vocabulary, is dry, and sometimes with one more twist than you might suppose: 'Wickham, perhaps, is my favourite; but I think I shall like *your* husband quite as well as Jane's.'[34] The first twist is that Mr Bennet is ironically turning his values upside down, with caddish Wickham at the top and delightful Bingley at the bottom. Accordingly, we would expect Darcy to be in the middle and dropping, but Mr Bennet twists again to leave that expectation defeated. What *can* he mean? George Bernard Shaw played the same game: 'With the single exception of Homer, there is no eminent writer, not even Sir Walter Scott, whom I can despise so entirely as I despise Shakespeare when I measure my mind against his.' If he had named only Homer and Shakespeare, he would be merely standing the facts on their head, but with the addition of poor Sir Walter—ah, there's the tang, the tease.

Elizabeth talks and jokes a lot, but not like this. Her sallies come in response to the words of other people, or solicit a response from them. Her humour also lies characteristically in content and ideas, rather than, as with her father, in diction and vocabulary. She mocks Darcy by claiming that he and she share the same turn of mind: 'We are each of an unsocial, taciturn disposition, unwilling to speak, unless we expect to say something that will amaze the whole room, and be handed down to posterity with all the eclat of a proverb.'[35] Of course she does not mean what she says, yet she actually speaks a truth: her humour is indeed social, and needs an audience. When she is talking to herself or thinking, she is actually rather solemn. The humour of Mrs Gardiner (related to the Bennets only by marriage) is a little different again, a broad, good-hearted banter: 'Pray forgive me, if I have been very presuming, or at least do not punish me so far, as to exclude me from P. I shall never be quite happy till I have been all round the park. A low phaeton, with a nice little pair of ponies, would be the very thing.'[36] But Mrs Gardiner, to be sure, is a character who is not much developed.

Whereas Elizabeth's humour is social, her father's seems often for himself alone. He seems hardly to care if anyone else understands his wit. The very first scene in the book, so gay, so funny, so famous, already indicates an emotional bleakness, in an undertone; for Mr Bennet is not bantering with his wife but privately laughing at her. Elizabeth and Darcy are never like this: there is a relationship, of a sort, between them from the start, even if it is a relationship of conflict. In the second chapter, when Mr Bennet reveals that he has after all gone to call on Bingley, his wife decides that he has been teasing her: ' "How good it was in you, my dear Mr Bennet! But I knew I should persuade you at last. I was sure you loved your girls too well to neglect such an acquaintance. Well, how pleased I am! And it is such a good joke, too, that you should have gone this morning, and never said a word about it till now." '[37] But we may suspect, after the first scene, that Mrs Bennet is too generous to her husband: he was not meaning to share a joke with her, but merely amusing himself.

Mr Bennet is one of Jane Austen's subtlest studies, and much of the subtlety resides in the way that his humour both defines his character and implicitly tells the history of his marriage. Mr and Mrs Palmer in *Sense and Sensibility* make a kind of rough sketch for a younger version of the Bennets: the silly, pretty wife who artlessly admires the cleverness of her sardonic, slightly eccentric husband. Whereas Mr Bennet is genuinely and inventively amusing, Palmer seems to be one of those people who suppose that the affectation of rudeness will be taken for wit; but the Palmers do suggest how the Bennets' marriage might have been before Mr Bennet began to find his wife tiresome and Mrs Bennet's young vivacity curdled. Mr Bennet uses humour as an emotional defence: 'Much as I abominate writing, I would not give up Mr. Collins's correspondence for any consideration. Nay, when I read a letter of his, I cannot help giving him the preference even over Wickham, much as I value the impudence and hypocrisy of my son-in-law.'[38] There is something rather dreadful about this. Mr Bennet should not be comparing Wickham with the oily Collins, not because he is a better man than Collins—he is indeed worse—but because his relationship to the family demands a more engaged response. Mr Bennet's response, though, is to keep him at an emotional distance, to flatten him into a butt so that he cannot hurt much. It is not unlike the way that he treats his wife. As we have seen, he has the self-knowledge to know that he tries to avoid self-knowledge: ' "No, Lizzy, let me once in my life feel how much I have been to blame. I am not afraid of being overpowered by the impression. It will pass away soon enough." '[39] Even in distress Mr Bennet keeps his wit; as a study of self-conflict this is very fine indeed.

Jane Austen lures us into the naughty pleasure of

laughing along with Mr Bennet. In her next novel she will show us the attractiveness of a naughty gaiety to a morally more complex end, in the depiction of Henry and Mary Crawford; it is desirable that we should like the Crawfords, so that we may appreciate both their moral possibilities and their dangerousness. We cannot help liking Mr Bennet, and blaming him less than we might. When his wife laments the prospect of living to see Charlotte Lucas as mistress of Longbourn, he replies, 'My dear, do not give way to such gloomy thoughts. Let us hope for better things. Let us flatter ourselves that *I* may be the survivor.'[40] This is one of Mr Bennet's weaker sallies, but it is brilliant on Jane Austen's part, for she here makes him reveal more than he means to, yet so lightly and briefly that we ourselves may hardly notice it. Desolation and emptiness lie not far below the surface; the implication is that Mr Bennet would find his wife's death a kind of comfort. To say this risks being too ponderous. I do not want to say that this book ceases being a comedy, or even that it ceases to sparkle. But as with some other great comedies, we may feel that only a little more weight in the pan might tip the balance towards something stark and terrible.

Mr Bennet's charm has sometimes seduced readers into believing him to be a spokesman for the book's own philosophy. 'For what do we live, but to make sport for our neighbours, and laugh at them in our turn'—this has been quoted as the expression of a ripe wisdom, a mature acceptance of the human comedy, something like the fugal chorus 'Tutto nel mondo burla' which ends Verdi's *Falstaff*.[41] But on reflection, it offers a bleak view of society and of human possibility (and in *Falstaff*, for that matter, it is not the few trite words of the libretto but the music which transfuses a sense of exhilaration and lovingly embraces the imperfection of our sublunary world). We should notice the circumstances which prompt Mr Bennet's remark: he has been trying to tease his favourite and most perceptive daughter and he is finding that a good joke is falling flat. A little hurt, he is attempting to retrieve his balance. Yet again we see the mastery of Jane Austen's portrait: everything he says always seems fitted to his personality and to the context.

In the last few years sequels to *Pride and Prejudice* and *Emma* have been commercially published (as well as a couple of completions of *Sanditon*). There are also said to be hundreds of Jane Austen sequels posted on the internet. This phenomenon does not seem to occur to the same degree with other classics, however popular—enthusiasts are not constantly speculating about what Angel Clare did next, or acclaiming Rodolfo's election to the Académie Française—so why does Jane attract this particular kind of homage? What is Elizabeth Bennet doing competing in cyberspace with Buffy Summers?

Daydreaming about the futures of fictional heroines may seem to be sentimental and unsophisticated, but the trouble with dismissing the game too sweepingly is that Jane Austen sometimes indulged in it herself. She wanted her niece Fanny to know that she had spotted a portrait of Mrs Bingley at an exhibition in London; she was disappointed not to see a picture of Mrs Darcy either there or at the Royal Academy, but reflected that it would be just like her husband's delicacy to keep it from promiscuous gaze.[42] And in answer to enquiry in the family, she revealed that Mr

Woodhouse died a couple of years after Emma's marriage. It would be wrong to make much of these private amusements; however, the temptation to treat the characters as real need not be altogether despised or even entirely resisted. We are indeed encouraged to feel that the characters continue to subsist after the book is ended.

The solid substance of her characters also makes it possible to pass judgements on them different from those of the author. Jane Austen deals in charm, the most elusive of literary qualities (if it were not elusive, it would surely not be charm?), and for many readers Elizabeth Bennet is the most charming heroine in fiction. But not quite everyone has liked her. Elizabeth Bowen, who praised Jane Austen for her power of creating charm, made an exception of Lizzy, whom she found definitely not charming; and Professor Gervase Fen, the detective in Edmund Crispin's whodunnits, listed among 'intolerable characters in fiction' ('the rule is that the author must have meant them to be attractive') 'those husband-hunting minxes in *Pride and Prejudice*'.[43] Most readers will disagree, but if we make the experiment of not liking Elizabeth Bennet, we may find that it does not matter to our appreciation of the book as much as we might have expected. She is enough like a real person for differing opinions of her reasonably to exist. Miss Bingley is a partial and prejudiced observer, but when she remarks on 'that little something, bordering on conceit and impertinence' which Elizabeth possesses, though we may dissent, we might allow that the judgement is not impossible.[44]

Some readers, however, may doubt whether Darcy is well enough conceived to withstand the same sort of treatment. It is with him that the highbrow and lower-middlebrow

attitudes to Jane Austen most diverge: much of her readership loves him, but the critics tend to think that he is not
entirely satisfactory. In terms of literary influence, he may
well be the most important of all her characters: at least,
most of the Mills and Boon heroes seem to fall into one of
three types: Darcy, Rochester (himself partly a variant of the
Darcy type), and Heathcliff. It is curious—or perhaps on
second thoughts not curious—that all three should have
been created by the maiden daughters of English parsons
within a period of less than fifty years. Because Darcy has
become a pop fantasy figure, he has been considered to be
something of a fantasy figure for the author herself—as it
were, the thinking woman's Lord Peter Wimsey.

One reason for his popularity is that he is the hero in
whom sexual desire is most overt and overpowering. For
what is he doing when he makes his first proposal to Elizabeth but telling her that he is so desperate to get her into bed
that he will marry her even though it will be a degradation to
him? The sexual charge is stronger in *Pride and Prejudice*
than in any of the other novels, and that is a proper part of its
character and appeal. But Darcy has also made a good
fantasy figure for his admirers because he is something of a
mystery. That is the significance of him. We know what
Lizzy is like, we see her close to, are admitted to her
thoughts. But a principal issue of the book is the question,
'What sort of man is Darcy?' Lizzy's exploration of this
question begins in a conversation between her and Wickham
which continues for several pages.[45] Wickham's quite elabo-
rate analysis of Darcy's character is fraudulent, but Elizabeth's interest in it is not. In another scene, a little later,
Darcy realizes that she is probing him:[46]

'May I ask to what these questions tend?'

'Merely to the illustration of *your* character,' said she, endeavouring to shake off her gravity. 'I am trying to make it out.'

'And what is your success?'

She shook her head. 'I do not get on at all. I hear such different accounts of you as puzzle me exceedingly.'

When she encounters him again on her visit to Kent, in company with his cousin Colonel Fitzwilliam, she is acute enough to realize that he must be different elsewhere from the silent man that he becomes in her presence;[47] she realizes that there is an undiscovered Darcy. The progress of the story shows her getting different accounts of him—from Wickham, from Colonel Fitzwilliam, from Mrs Reynolds, the housekeeper at Pemberley. Mrs Reynolds herself is aware that there are divergent views of him. 'Some people call him proud', but she has seen nothing of it. 'To my fancy, it is only because he does not rattle away like other young men.'[48] It has been objected that on his first appearance, at the ball, Darcy is a sneering milord, a figure incompatible with the great gentleman who emerges later on. But that objection only has force if Darcy is taken to be a flat character. On this occasion he is in a thoroughly bad mood, and the mistake that Elizabeth and the others make is to assume that Darcy in a rotten temper is the only Darcy that there is.

It is also an assumption that the question about Darcy's character is, or should be, completely answered at the end of the book. It may still be possible, within limits, to speculate. Mrs Gardiner, late in the novel, has her view: 'I fancy, Lizzy, that obstinacy is the real defect of his character. He has been accused of many faults at different times; but *this* is the true one.'[49] Well, that is one judgement, and it comes from a pretty shrewd judge. The book is called *Pride and Prejudice*, but the two principals are not, after all, symmetrically treated. The scheme is that we should see Darcy through others' eyes. That is why the leading man in this theatrical novel has, paradoxically, proved so difficult to adapt for stage and screen. Louis Menand has wittily observed that the BBC's last adaptation was a faithful version of Jane Austen's novel 'with added Darcy'. So we saw him taking a bath, fencing, catching Wickham *in flagrante* with a floozy, and so on—scenes characteristic of the cinema rather than the stage. But in fact Jane Austen's treatment of Darcy is entirely 'theatrical'—that is, we only hear him speaking. The problem for actors and adapters comes from the expectation that the leading man should be treated on an equal footing with the leading lady. But that is not what Jane Austen designed. It is not a fault that Darcy is blurry as Elizabeth is not, or that as a study of character he is less complex and subtle. On the contrary, it adds to the novel's range and realism, and the diversity of its pleasures. We are to understand her, and to wonder about him.

We might agree that at least some elements in the depiction of Darcy are very good. Here are two touches of psychological perception which are particularly nice. When Elizabeth rejects his proposal, he evidently feels anger, humiliation, and sexual frustration; and he has been accused of dastardly behaviour (towards Wickham) of which he is entirely innocent. But there is another, more particular pain. Lizzy tells him that he has not behaved in a gentleman-like manner and 'She saw him start at this.'[50] Much later, after she has accepted him, he can analyse his more essentially moral faults—selfishness, pride, and conceit—with calmness. Indeed, he is probably being too hard on himself here, and perhaps that is why he can be philosophically serene about the matter: the pleasures of pride and self-esteem may be indulged even within the act of repentance, and there is some gratification in the thought that another will think of us better than we think of ourselves. But his failure in terms of his own social code—that very code whose imperfection and limitations he thinks he has discovered—is an agony to him:[51]

> Your reproof, so well applied, I shall never forget: 'had you behaved in a more gentleman-like manner.' Those were your words. You know not, you can scarcely conceive, how they have tortured me; . . .

He minds more that he has failed in his own terms than that those terms are wrong. And this rings entirely true. Gwen Raverat describes in her memoir of childhood, *Period Piece*, how she perceived as a girl that the grown-ups had two moral systems: there was the Christian code of virtue, which they said was by far the more important, and there was also the code of 'ladies and gentlemen', which actually counted for most. She also noticed that shame for an action, possibly well meaning, which had gone embarrassingly awry tended to be a more potent and painful emotion than guilt for a deliberate wrong. These perceptions apply well to *Pride and Prejudice*: it is the unintended part of the wrong in his conduct to Elizabeth that has tormented Darcy most.

The betrothal duet between Elizabeth and Darcy ends with him explaining how he has confessed to Bingley and been forgiven:[52]

Elizabeth longed to observe that Mr. Bingley had been a most delightful friend; so easily guided that his worth was invaluable; but she checked herself. She remembered that he had yet to learn to be laught at, and it was rather too early to begin.

This, it might be said, tells us most about Elizabeth's character: playful and acute, she will not allow her love for Darcy to blind her to the continued limitations of his personality. But it tells us about Darcy too: a certain stiffness and solemnity remain with him. It also looks forward to the nature of his marriage and at the same time reminds us that he is going through a process of development that is not yet complete when the action of the novel comes to its end. Knightley and Wentworth are going to have wholly admiring wives, by the look of it, but the marriage of Mr and Mrs Darcy will be different. On the last page of the book we learn that Darcy's sister is at first alarmed at the sportive way in which Elizabeth addresses him but is then liberated by seeing him 'the object of open pleasantry'. She is liberated by this; but so, surely, is he. Again, we learn something of his character from the fact that he will, in due course, like to be teased. It reveals his fundamental virtue. As Elizabeth herself has told him, he has been wearied by the adulation he has received from others, and been drawn to her 'impertinence'.[53]

The final explanation of Mr Darcy is provided from his own mouth:[84]

I have been a selfish being all my life, in practice, though not in principle. As a child I was taught what was *right*, but I was not taught to correct my temper. I was given good principles, but left to follow them in pride and conceit. Unfortunately an only son, (for many years an only *child*) I was spoilt by my parents, who though all good themselves, (my father particularly, all that was benevolent and amiable,) allowed, encouraged, almost taught me to be selfish and overbearing, to care for none beyond my own family circle, to think meanly of all the rest of the world, to *wish* at least to think meanly of their sense and worth compared with my own. Such I was, from eight to eight and twenty; and such I might still have been but for you, dearest, loveliest Elizabeth! What do I not owe you! You taught me a lesson, hard indeed at first, but most advantageous. By you, I was properly humbled.

We can see from this that two things, the unfolding of Darcy's real character and the development of that character, are carefully planned by the author. Yet one may still feel that there is something here that is not entirely satisfying. It still needs Mr Darcy to explain what Mr Darcy is: ideally that should not be necessary. Whereas Elizabeth and her father, for example, are fully realized in their words and actions, Darcy is perhaps not—not quite.

We may also feel that the relationship between Elizabeth and her father is perhaps more interesting, more subtly and penetratingly realized, than that between her and Darcy. In this case, however, I do not think that we should complain of a flaw in the book's moral balance. There would be a flaw if Darcy and Elizabeth were the joint protagonists of the story, but they are not. This is Elizabeth's book, and his first function is to be the object of her changing judgements and sentiments. It is indeed part of the book's psychological truthfulness that her relation to Mr Bennet has a closeness and complexity that her relation to her lover does not. In the future that will no doubt change, but in the present it must be so.

4

A Park with a View

Mansfield Park is the book which divides Jane Austen's readers most. It is reputed to be the least popular of her novels, and some people dislike it quite strongly: Kingsley Amis, in a notorious attack, called it a corrupted book and pronounced its hero and heroine morally detestable (a little rich, one may think, from an author whose third novel—reputedly his favourite—advocates rape as a good way of overcoming a girlfriend's modesty).[1] Less intemperately, many readers have felt that Edmund and Fanny are too priggish, or perhaps that Jane Austen herself has turned prig. There seems to be almost universal agreement that Fanny is an unsatisfactory heroine. But it is also generally acknowledged that the novel is in most respects extraordinarily accomplished (Amis himself thought that there was much to be said for the view that it was Jane Austen's best book, and he disliked it in part for going about its wicked work with such brilliance). Most of those who know Jane

Austen best appear to regard *Mansfield Park* as a masterpiece, a deep book.

I share the view that *Mansfield Park* is a very great novel. But I want to go further. I think that it is not far from being a perfect novel. Most rashly, I shall suggest that the treatment of the heroine is masterly and profound: Fanny Price may stand comparison with Emma Woodhouse. Indeed the two are appropriately set side by side, for each is a study, in very different circumstances and upon very different personalities, of the effects of repression. But the Fanny problem (as it seems to so many readers to be) is best approached after considering the book's form and rhythm, its distinctive colour and tone. What kind of book is it? Should we indeed class it as a comedy at all?

A difficulty which very few artists have had to confront is how to follow perfection, and in particular comic perfection. Mozart faced it after *The Marriage of Figaro*. In this opera he had composed a virtually perfect comedy of manners, with at the same time a deep humanity. Its perfection, as with *Pride and Prejudice*, is not only a happy characteristic but part of its essence: at the heart of the aesthetic experience is the enjoyment, among other things, of a wonderful piece of machinery. Such a thing could not be repeated, and indeed Mozart never wrote another opera with that special quality of perfection. Where could he go next? The issue is complicated in the case of music drama by the fact that the composer is dependent on what the librettist can be persuaded to produce, but on this occasion Lorenzo da Ponte surely gave him what he needed. *Don Giovanni* is not a less great work than *Figaro*, and it is indeed fabulously accomplished, but it is essentially puzzling and strange. Yet its oddness does not mark a regression on the composer's part: it was the necessary way forward.

Shakespeare faced the same issue after *Twelfth Night*. He followed it not with comedies of an even more perfected mellowness, but with the problem plays. *Mansfield Park* is Jane Austen's problem novel, and as with *Don Giovanni* and *Measure for Measure* we may perhaps reckon it to be a comedy, but only just. After the perfection of *Pride and Prejudice* she tries a new tone; *Mansfield Park* is essentially odd and uneasy, and fittingly so. It is an experimental novel in various respects, most strikingly in the intertextual relationship with the play *Lovers' Vows*. No one would read this tripe now but for *Mansfield Park*, and even at the time Jane Austen can hardly have expected all her public to know the work, yet it undoubtedly enhances our appreciation of quite a large part of the novel to have read it—a curious kind of demand on the reader. She also experiments with touches of symbolism and develops a new sense of the significance of place; and she dares to invent a very unusual type of heroine. A surprising number of critics in effect take *Emma* as the type of the Austen novel, and judge the others by the extent to which they match or fail to match that pattern; but whether we judge her to have succeeded or not in *Mansfield Park* (and I myself think that she succeeds magnificently), we should at least recognize in it the ambition to strike out on a new and original path.

The book's distinctive tone is exemplified in the treatment of Mrs Norris and Sir Thomas Bertram. In terms of form and structure, Mrs Norris plays a dominant role in *Mansfield Park*: she is the first person to speak in it and her first extended utterance is longer than any speech of Fanny's in the entire novel. That is fitting: Mrs Norris makes her debut like the wicked fairy at the christening, and she will harry the heroine remorselessly for nine years until her final defeat at the book's end. She may not be quite the nastiest person in the novels (that honour should go to Mrs John Dashwood, or perhaps to General Tilney, though because of the predominantly genial tone of *Northanger Abbey* he tends to get forgotten), but she is so presented as to be the most hateful. Yet she might also seem deserving of pity. Hers has been a wretched history of disappointed hopes. Once pretty, she failed to catch a good husband, and 'found herself obliged to be attached' to a clergyman without money. He is an invalid, and dies early (he may well have been a good deal older than she). She has no children, and seems likely to have been sexually frustrated.

The frustration of her maternal instinct is more clearly indicated, most obviously in her unnaturally and unhealthily passionate attachment to her eldest niece. But there are other hints. It may be significant that she has a servant called Nanny—a diminutive of Anne, but a name that was already established as a title for a children's nurse. When Fanny is back with her chaotic family in Portsmouth, the author, with her usual feeling for family likenesses, notes that Mrs Price resembles her sister Lady Bertram in having a 'naturally easy and indolent disposition', and would have turned out much like Lady Bertram had she married as well. But the other sister is quite different: '[Mrs Price] was a manager by necessity without any of Mrs. Norris's inclination for it, or any of her activity . . . Mrs Norris would have been a more respectable mother of nine children, on a small income.'[2] This is an unexpected thought, but it rings true. It is hard to imagine Mrs Norris as a charming mother, but she might have been by most lights a good one, and fulfilled in that role. Two frustrations are suggested here: the lack of children, and the lack of any vent for her natural energy. Very early on, in fact, Jane Austen says, explicitly, that her passion for penny-pinching is the consequence of a vigour denied its wholesome outlet: 'she had, from the first, fancied a very strict line of economy necessary; and what was begun as a matter of prudence soon grew into a matter of choice as an object of that needful solicitude which there were no children to supply. Had there been a family to provide for, Mrs Norris might never have saved her money; . . .'[3] It is worth noting how here in the first chapter we are told that, with a little more luck in life, Mrs Norris might have been a quite different person. None other of Jane Austen's 'baddies'— Wickham, Lucy Steele, General Tilney, Mrs Elton, William Elliot—has been tried as she has.

Mrs Norris is a damaged personality, the only character in the six novels who might plausibly be suspected of psychological disturbance. Her behaviour is obsessive: she may be naturally mean, but such small details as her capture of the green baize used for the play (she carries it off to her cottage) show the hunter-gatherer instinct hypertrophically developed.[4] There is something obsessive too about her persecution of small children. Fanny, of course, she bullies relentlessly. But there is also a tiny episode, told by herself, of how she bullied a 10-year-old boy (again in a tussle over some material of very small value—this time a couple of deal boards).[5] Little Dick Jackson, whose only existence is in Mrs Norris's account of him, is one of those off-stage characters whose presence is oddly substantial.[6]

Mrs Norris has nobody to love her, or even to care for her. We never learn her Christian name; why should it ever be wanted? It may be doubted whether she has even the sad pleasure of loving without return: her fixation upon the Bertram sisters can hardly be called love. And evidently she has not loved her late husband. The best anyone seems to feel for her is indifference; to most she is plainly the object of disdain or dislike. Even the butler is allowed to smile sarcastically at her—one of the very rare moments in Jane Austen when a servant's viewpoint counts.[7] Fanny alone is allowed (a little) to pity her, but even she can feel no regret at all when Mrs Norris departs. It is a terrible condition, this utter lovelessness, shared by no other character in the six novels.

Lovelessness, in less extreme form, is, however, a condition recurrent in *Mansfield Park*, and it is perhaps this more than anything that gives the book its cold, clear, desolate character. Sir Thomas Bertram, despite his essential virtue, is almost as little loved as his sister-in-law. The child Fanny, though she knows that she ought to feel affection for him, guiltily realizes that she cannot: he is simply too stiff and forbidding. His daughters are more at ease when he is away from home:[8]

> Their father was no object of love to them, he had never seemed the friend of their pleasures, and his absence was unhappily most welcome. They were relieved by it from all restraint; and without aiming at one gratification that would probably have been forbidden by Sir Thomas, they felt themselves immediately at their own disposal, and to have every indulgence within their reach.

Something rather similar is said about another character in one of the other novels: in *Northanger Abbey* Catherine, along with the younger Tilneys, feels the relief when General Tilney leaves the house—'every laugh indulged', the ease and good humour, 'pleasures and fatigues at their own command, made her thoroughly sensible of the restraint which the General's presence had imposed, and most thankfully feel their present release from it'.[9] Hard is the fate that leads Sir Thomas's effect to be described in language so like that applied to an especially nasty figure. It is a subtle touch that Sir Thomas's presence is not felt by his daughters as preventing them from any particular pleasure but as a general formless repressiveness; they are not depraved, or longing for adventure, or even lively, but merely breathing in an atmosphere of dull stuffiness. Even to contemplate their father's return to England casts a gloom over them,[10] and when he actually arrives, unexpectedly, nobody greets his coming with pleasure except his wife; indeed, most of the company are horrified. 'Poor Sir Thomas,' says Mary Crawford, looking back much later upon that sombre evening, 'who was glad to see you?'—and that light contempt, that easy passing pity show us how grimly Jane Austen might have chosen to paint his condition.[11]

Like Mr Bennet's, his marriage is pretty much dead. In *Pride and Prejudice* the deadness of the marriage is very plainly shown; in *Mansfield Park*, that most subtle, stealthy novel, the awareness creeps upon us almost imperceptibly; nowhere is the truth quite directly spoken. But Lady Bertram, in Henry Crawford's mind, 'might always be considered as only half awake';[12] she cannot provide companionship for a rational and honourable man, even one of so limited an imagination as Sir Thomas. Even before his absence in Antigua, they have lived a good deal apart: several years before the main action of the book begins, she has given up accompanying him to London, so that he has to do his parliamentary business without her, 'with whatever increase or diminution of comfort might arise from her absence'. On a later occasion we find that he would rather not play cards at all than have her for a partner.[13] When he is crossing the seas, and at some danger, she is unable to worry about him, as her indolence—of mind as much as body—renders her incapable of much feeling for other people, or for anything beyond her immediate sight. Jane Austen has a sense of the unknowable privacy and inwardness of the marriage relation. She disclaims the novelist's omniscience and allows an area of uncertainty: 'whatever increase or diminution of comfort *might* arise', '*might perhaps* feel that it would not much amuse him to have her for a partner'. But on the happiest estimate, Sir Thomas's marriage cannot be deeply fulfilling.

After disaster has struck, Jane Austen in her summing up will echo in her own serious voice the phrase that Mary Crawford has so lightly used: 'Sir Thomas, poor Sir Thomas . . . was the longest to suffer.'[14] He is of the stuff to make a tragic figure. He fits the Aristotelian idea of the imperfectly but essentially good man who suffers in consequence of a mistake or error. His very virtue—his desire to impose a solemn and orderly decorum upon his family—has by the repression of their natural spirits been the means of leading his children astray. And his virtuous self-knowledge is the very instrument of his suffering: it is because he is 'a parent, and conscious of errors in his own conduct as a parent' that he is so anguished. His wife, a far more defective parent, is quite incapable of suffering in this way: she has not the merit for it.

100

But it is very fine that Jane Austen will not make him tragic. That was Fanny's idea: she supposes that it will be scarcely possible for him and Edmund to 'support life and reason under such disgrace', but Edmund corrects this impression: 'My father is not overpowered.'[15] Sir Thomas's stoicism imposes itself upon the narrative, so that we are able to pity him less than we might have thought. It is a mark of great artistry that Jane Austen should deepen her story by making us feel, in this respect, not more but less.

The handling of Mrs Norris at the end is more similar to this than we might have expected. Mrs Norris is not a caricature but a deep study of an extreme personality, who might have developed differently if circumstances had been kinder, and in the last chapter she is able to surprise us, yet in a way that is entirely consistent with her character. Her obsessive fondness for Mrs Rushworth leads her into an act of lasting self-sacrifice: 'It ended in Mrs. Norris's resolving to quit Mansfield, and devote herself to her unfortunate Maria, and in an establishment being formed for them in another country—remote and private, . . .'[16] It is easy to pass this moment by as just a device for punishing the villain and completing the happy ending, but that is to underestimate the author. For after all, Mrs Norris's sacrifice is self-chosen. And for the first time in her life she has a worthwhile purpose to perform.

But just as Jane Austen will not make Sir Thomas tragic, so she wonderfully resists the temptation to redeem Mrs Norris. Almost any other novelist who had thought of the brilliant idea of Mrs Norris's voluntary self-immolation would have gone a little further: we should have learnt that the lady found some solace in being of service to another (and we might perhaps have heard Mrs Rushworth, like Little Em'ly, weeping ceaseless tears of gratifying penitence). That is not Jane Austen's way. Let us complete the quotation: '... where, shut up together with little society, on one side no affection, on the other, no judgment, it may be reasonably supposed that their tempers became their mutual punishment.' Jane Austen knows that it is right to maintain the brutal tone. I am tempted to a lofty comparison: at the end of the *Aeneid*, Virgil's hero has his foe Turnus at his feet. Aeneas thinks for a moment of mercy, but then, reminded of one of the young men whom Turnus has slain, plunges his weapon into his enemy's body in passionate anger. Even if it is right for Turnus to die, Virgil could easily have made his killer more magnanimous in spirit, more regretful in action; but he knows that it is right aesthetically and psychologically—perhaps in a sense even morally—to preserve an element that is hard and unrelenting.

However, to say that Jane Austen dismisses Mrs Norris to a permanent and unrelieved purgatory is to tell not quite the whole story. The words 'it may be reasonably supposed' are not redundant: these people have passed beyond our range of vision, beyond the range even of the author's omniscience. She has allowed us to make our own estimate of when Edmund was ready to transfer his affections to Fanny, and the way in which she dismisses Maria and her aunt from the story admits, in theory, the possibility that their fate was not quite as grim as appears likely. But it is hardly more than a theoretical possibility, for the reasons which Jane Austen has so harshly spelled out; the balance between indeterminacy and a sense of ruthless closure is very finely maintained. There will be no overt word of sympathy or respect for Mrs

Norris, and almost all readers seem to have followed almost all the people at Mansfield Park in feeling no pity for her; but apart from Fanny, there is, I think, at least one person who pities her: Jane Austen.

Given the subfusc coloration of *Mansfield Park* as a whole, the bright, facetious tone with which the last chapter opens may seem surprising: 'Let other pens dwell on guilt and misery. I quit such odious subjects as soon as I can, impatient to restore every body, not greatly in fault themselves, to tolerable comfort, and have done with all the rest.' Or compare—what might have been the subject of half a novel—the change in Edmund's affections, introduced rather late even within the final chapter:[17]

> I purposely abstain from dates on this occasion, that every one may be at liberty to fix their own, aware that the cure of unconquerable passions, and the transfer of unchanging attachments, must vary much as to time in different people.—I only intreat every body to believe that exactly at the time when it was quite natural that it should be so, and not a week earlier, Edmund did cease to care about Miss Crawford, and became as anxious to marry Fanny, as Fanny herself could desire.

Where have we heard this tart, pert note before? In *Northanger Abbey*, and hardly since then. It belongs with the light, half-farcical tone of that novel that the author should break the illusion of naturalism, and remind us that she is inventing and controlling the story—or to put it another way, that the book is a book and not life: 'The anxiety . . . can hardly extend, I fear, to the bosom of my readers, who will see in the tell-tale compression of the pages before them, that we are all hastening together to perfect felicity.'[18] The twentieth century has invented the term 'alienation effect' and provided it with a highbrow context, but historically it has been a device belonging mostly to the lower genres of literature. The characters in Greek tragedy never appeal to the audience sitting in the theatre or make overt allusions to contemporary events; the characters in Aristophanes often do. In pantomime Widow Twankey inhabits ancient China and modern England at the same time, and the Ugly Sisters make jokes about television commercials. In *Northanger Abbey* Jane Austen may draw attention to the fictionality of her fiction, but even in *Pride and Prejudice*, as light of spirit as *Northanger Abbey* and more sparkling, such a device is avoided, as it would compromise the story's naturalism. Yet here it is returning in the more sombre *Mansfield Park*.

'Let other pens dwell on guilt and misery'—apart from the question of tone, the declaration seems to run counter to the rest of a book which has dwelt more on guilt and misery than any other of Jane Austen's works. Fanny herself spends almost all of it in low spirits, and there is less space for comedy than in the other novels. Lady Bertram, perhaps the best candidate for a 'comic' character, is hardly more than half alive—that is the point of her. And Mrs Norris is too bitterly etched to be comic in the ordinary sense; and besides being odious, she is a study of profound unhappiness—no lack of misery there. Yet paradoxically, the sudden inflow of facetiousness, with its distancing effect, actually confirms the sombre character of the book as whole, for it gives the last chapter the feeling of an epilogue or postscript. As I have already suggested, the action of the story seems to end with a kind of stalemate: the Crawfords have been seen off, but Maria is ruined and the other Bertrams left bereft; Edmund is certain that he can never care for another woman again, and so Fanny seems to be no nearer to happiness. And there, in effect, the curtain comes down. The brisk style of the final chapter sounds like the kind of tidying up with which so many eighteenth- and nineteenth-century novels end: the account, if it can be called that, of Edmund and Fanny's courtship feels like the information that the Bingleys moved to the north of England or that Marianne eventually grew deeply fond of Colonel Brandon. In terms of the drama before us, it seems like a glimpse into the future.

The last chapter also contains a death, that of the parson, Dr Grant, and elsewhere deaths in Jane Austen's novels (contrary to a widespread belief, several are recorded) are always in some sense off-stage and outside the action: they occur before the action of the story begins, or, as with the death of Frank Churchill's aunt, some hundreds of miles away from the scene before our eyes. Dr Grant's decease is unique in the novels in that it is the death of someone who, if not quite one of the dramatis personae, is present at the scene of the action and is known to all the main characters; it is thus, in formal terms, another indication that the story is over, and that the author is mopping up after the curtain fall. The death is also broadly comic ('brought on . . . by three great institutionary dinners in one week'). Try it as a quiz question: in which classic English novel does someone drop dead after repeatedly guzzling too much in one week? Few will guess Jane Austen, and least of all *Mansfield Park*. Here again she has adopted a manner different from the rest of the book, another indication that the action is complete, and that we have relaxed into the different style of an after- word. At the close of *Don Giovanni*, after the protagonist's unrepentant descent to hell, some brisk, bright ensemble music assures us that the opera buffa has come to a properly happy ending. In a way, this moves the balance of feeling back to comedy; yet it seems too perfunctory to cancel the darkness that has gone before. In terms of the balance of feeling the technique at the end of *Mansfield Park* bears a resemblance to this.

Those who think that Jane Austen went sour in *Mansfield Park* have sometimes attributed the change to some disturbance in her life or opinions. In general, rather few critics have resisted the temptation to bring her own life to bear on the study of her work, and since we do know a good deal about her, it would indeed be unnatural to pretend to an ignorance which we lack the power to regain. In seeking to interpret any writer we might try to maintain two principles: first, that it is worth finding out what we can about his life, partly as a check on what we believe his purposes to have been, partly in the hope of illuminating aspects of his work which we might otherwise have missed; and second, that ultimately we have to believe the work itself. Of course, there is *some* relationship between an author's personality and his work, but we cannot assume that such relationship is direct and straightforward. Derangement provides an interesting test: in some cases we may suspect from the work that its creator was mentally disturbed, but who would guess, for example, Hugo Wolf's history from his music? It is also wrong to assume that the whole of an artist's personality is in his productions; in reality, he may hold a great deal in reserve. We might suppose that Burne-Jones was languid and wholly lacking in humour but for the accidental survival of a few caricature drawings showing exceptional wit and vigour of line. Lord Berners was a composer, writer, and painter; in his music he was a modernist, but his landscapes were attractive in a thoroughly traditional style. Gerard Manley Hopkins was an avant-garde poet but a traditional draughtsman; and the modernism of Joyce's prose contrasts with the late-romantic melancholy of his verses.

Some writers are particularly prone to being interpreted in terms of what we might call the simple biographical method. Almost universally, Shakespeare's sonnets are taken as direct reports on the private life of William Shakespeare, although there was a craze for sequences of love sonnets in the 1590s, which are otherwise agreed to be largely or entirely fictitious. Among twentieth-century authors, T. S. Eliot has been perhaps the most notable object of the simple biographical method, principally because of our age's sensitivity about anti-Semitism. Yet it should be obvious that the young Eliot put on a number of masks—sarcastic, bitter, anti-clerical, effete. The ironic title of *Mr Eliot's Sunday Morning Service* should be enough to indicate to the reader that the relationship between 'Mr Eliot' and the historical Thomas Stearns Eliot is at best elusive and oblique, that the etiolated and oversophisticated voice of the poem issues from a persona which has been consciously assumed. In most cases critics well understand the importance of separating the persona—merely the Latin word for 'mask'—from the historical person of the author, but with early Eliot an external pressure—in this case, concern about racial prejudice and persecution—has sometimes been allowed to override critical discipline.

Jane Austen may seem to have little in common with

Eliot—except for a strong Anglican piety—but one may suspect that in her case too there are pressures which cause ordinary critical circumspection to break down. One of these is the peculiar affection in which the person of Jane Austen is held by many readers. People feel that they are acquainted with her, and that they are meeting her, not only in her letters or in the story of her life, but as much or more in her fiction. Jane herself is speaking to us, we may be tempted to think, and we can always recognize her voice. And there is another, more insidious pressure, on which I have already touched: the supposition, accepted by many of her admirers and assumed by her detractors, that there is little variety in her. If you think that the novels are straightforwardly the expressions of Miss Austen's personality, you are indeed likely to suppose that her moral outlook underwent a considerable change shortly before she began *Mansfield Park*. If you believe that the books are slight variations on a single theme, you are likely to think that the author of *Pride and Prejudice* has lost her way. 'Is this still Jane Austen?' in Kingsley Amis's wailing words. 'What became of Jane Austen?'

My answer is that nothing became of her at all: she simply chose to write a different kind of book. This argument must be made from the novels themselves, but it does get some support from the chronology of her works. If *Mansfield Park* had come after *Emma*, it would be easier to suppose a darkening or hardening of Jane Austen's moral idea in the later part of her life. But in *Emma*, so close to *Mansfield Park* in date, she returns to brilliancy and exhilaration and to broadly comic characters (Mrs Elton, Miss Bates). Indeed, I shall suggest that it is illuminating to take these two novels as a pair, both parallel and contrasting. Some critics, though, would argue that whatever Jane Austen's intentions may have been, *Mansfield Park* is wounded by an inadequacy at its centre. It is time to confront the protagonist.

Jane Austen once declared that she was 'going to take a heroine that no one but myself will much like'.[19] She was referring to Emma, but for many modern readers it is Fanny Price who fits the description best. That may tell us something about changing tastes and mores: the Victorians were too fond of the meekly perfect heroine; we, on the other hand, may be too reluctant to admire goodness, especially when it takes the form of passive, unspectacular endurance. I hope to avoid the trap of awarding marks for moral superiority to those who find Fanny likeable, but it is perhaps worth noting that both the men in Fanny's life, Henry and Edmund, take quite a while to see her as an object of desire. With all the other heroines, the man's physical attraction to her is immediate or even antecedent to the beginning of the story. Fanny Price takes some getting to know. For what it is worth, my own experience has been that the longer one lives with *Mansfield Park*, the more lovable she becomes.

Certainly, in choosing someone like Fanny Price for a heroine, Jane Austen is taking a risk. Though the meekly virtuous heroine is common enough in the Victorian novel, she appears most often as a subsidiary character, who has nothing much to do but wait for the hero to bestow upon her the privilege of his love. Where she is expected to take the principal role, as in *Little Dorrit* or *Bleak House*, she becomes a drag upon the book: Esther Summerson is a serious defect in *Bleak House*, through Dickens's ill-judged decision to make this drippily sweet character narrate a large part of the story; and if Amy Dorrit does not do much damage in the later novel, it is because, as so often in Dickens, the notionally central characters are rather less important than the lively world that swirls around them. Jane Austen's self-imposed challenge is to make the good little mouse the very heart of the story.

C. S. Lewis, in an essay of characteristic eloquence and charm, argued that the challenge was one which she was bound to fail.[20] 'One of the most dangerous of literary ventures,' he wrote, 'is the little, shy, unimportant heroine whom none of the other characters value. The danger is that your readers may agree with the other characters.' That is entirely true: the danger is indeed great, and the fact that so many readers have been dissatisfied with Fanny Price confirms it. But Lewis goes a step further: it is essential, he argues, that the author should show the 'other characters' to be wrong by finding depths in the mousy heroine that they are unaware of. Fanny fails (on this account) because she has nothing to counterbalance her apparent insignificance except rectitude—'neither passion, nor physical courage, nor wit, nor resource'. So to write a book around such a heroine is not merely to court danger, it seems; it is a kamikaze mission.

I should be reluctant to concede so much. It has been one of the boasts of the novel that it does not restrict itself to the splendours and miseries of the grand, the glamorous, and the clever; all human life, however ordinary and unspectacular, comes within its purview. Thackeray wrote ironically about the idea that fate was 'of an aristocratic turn', delighting in combat with such princely families as the Bourbons or the House of Atreus, 'the Browns and Joneses being of no account'.[21] George Eliot explained in *Adam Bede* that she was composing a 'Dutch painting' in prose, with the purpose of revealing that commonplace joys and sorrows, the lives of plain, homely people were as interesting and significant as the lives of the great.[22] Plenty of people are dull or insignificant or lacking in talent and resource. If they cannot play a leading role in a work of literature, we must conclude that there is much that literature cannot do. Undoubtedly, it would have been easier to have made Fanny seethe with passion or rebellion under the surface. That is the easy solution taken in Patricia Rozema's film of *Mansfield Park*, but it does violence to the whole tenor of the book. For if Jane Austen fails with Fanny, it is not through inadvertence; of that we can surely be confident. If it is impossible for any author to make someone like Fanny succeed as a heroine, then Jane Austen must indeed fail. But if a 'storm of passion' had blown through Fanny (Lewis's suggestion of how she would have been if Charlotte Brontë were writing the book), she would not have been Fanny, and the book would not have been *Mansfield Park*.

For dullness is the essence of the book: it is a study of dullness. Fanny is dull, at least to outward appearance. Edmund is dull, even though sweet-natured. Sir Thomas is decent but dull. Lady Bertram is not only boring but too bored almost to stir from her sofa. Nice Mrs Grant is so bored in the Mansfield parsonage that she longs for her half-sister's arrival and worries only that Mary may find the place too uninteresting.[23] Henry's absence from Mansfield for a mere couple of weeks produces 'a fortnight of such dulness to the Bertrams as ought to have put them both on their guard', and after Sir Thomas's return, even Edmund feels the 'want of animation' in the family and the heaviness with which the evenings pass. Fanny correctly notes that this is nothing new: there was never much laughter when Sir Thomas was around, and the evenings were never merry. She assumes this is the usual condition in a family when the father is present.[24] Jane Austen's own books give her the lie: in all the other novels, somewhere or other, there is a clutch of noisy, lively children.

It is because the Park is so dull that the ordinary worldliness of the Crawfords can disturb it so profoundly. After all, Henry is not good looking—indeed the first reaction of the Bertram girls is that he is distinctly plain—but he will succeed in seducing one of them because he can offer what is so desperately lacking at Mansfield Park: fun. The play is so disruptive because it overexcites the young people: Jane Austen represents very accurately the breaking out of an animation that has been too much damped down. Boredom in Jane Austen could be the subject of a book in itself: all the novels, including *Northanger Abbey*, depict the corrosive effect on the leisured classes, especially on women, of a lack of scope for their energies or a deficiency in useful or improving activity. It is an important element in *Emma*, but in *Mansfield Park* it is all pervasive.

I suspect that Jane Austen may have been trying to test the limits, to see how far she could go. Deliberately she withdraws from her heroine most of the attractions that might compensate for her timidity: Fanny is made to have no interest in music or drawing; she says that she does not want to learn them.[25] Conversely, the author has made Mary Crawford the character most like herself, indeed along with Lizzy Bennet the character in all the novels most like herself. Mary seems to resemble her creator in physical appearance, and certainly she does so in her musicality, wit, and liveliness, and in the risqué freedom of her epistolary style. It is a subtlety of the book, not an inadvertence on the part of a priggish, clumsy author, that the reader is tempted, in the same way that the inhabitants of Mansfield Park are tempted, to see the Crawfords as the salvation of the place's repressive dullness and to write off poor dim Fanny. It is a mark of Jane Austen's literary courage and breadth of moral imagination that she makes the Crawfords not, like Wickham or William Elliot, spuriously attractive, but genuinely so: they have real charm, warmth, and affectionate natures; they possess moral perception and possibility. In one respect, the modern reader is likely to side with Mary where the bulk of the original readership, like the principal characters, will not have done. At the end of the story Mary argues that the Rushworths' marriage is finished, and that the best thing will be for the family to encourage them to divorce and try to get Henry to marry Maria.[26] Here the common worldly wisdom of the twenty-first century is with her (she is too sanguine in hoping that Henry will go along with the plan, but that is another issue, and anyway she is pretty well aware of it herself), but Edmund's utter opposition is his proper response as an orthodox Christian priest, for whom marriage is an unbreakable vow, and he is right to be repelled by Mary's unawareness of his deeply held principles, or her indifference to them: despite her love for him, this amounts to a form of contempt.

Fanny's detractors find her too censorious, and certainly she observes narrowly and assigns blame where blame is due. There are reasons of literary economy for this. Fanny takes the part of the implied narrator; hers are the eyes through which the action is seen. So she needs to be a sharp judge. We can see from other novels what happens if the sweet observing heroine has no dash of acid in her. Esther Summerson, as the narrator of much of *Bleak House*, is required to tell us about a number of disagreeable people, like the cadging, canting Harold Skimpole. Dickens always had a tendency to confuse virtue with simple-mindedness, an error seen at its worst in *Martin Chuzzlewit*, where Tom Pinch's rosy view of Mr Pecksniff comes near to imbecility; and Esther accordingly has to describe Skimpole in terms that make clear to us that he is a scoundrel, while being wholly or largely unaware of it herself. Dickens implicitly proposes that she is simply too charitable to spot badness in others; but we are likely to feel merely that she is a fool, not morally adult. I have referred earlier to the twentieth century's fondness for the 'unreliable narrator' and the difficulty of using this device with success: the risk is that the author will condescend to his creations. What Jane Austen's plot requires, at all events, is a reliable narrator, one whose judgements are sharp in both senses of the word—who cuts accurately and cuts keen. I do not mean to say that Fanny's judgement or her character is flawless. Most critics seem to assume that her views are exactly those of the author; I shall try to argue that this is not so.

When he starts to get interested in her, Henry Crawford remarks, 'I do not quite know what to make of Miss Fanny. I do not understand her . . . What is her character?—Is she solemn?—Is she queer?—Is she prudish?'[27] Like Henry, who is a shrewd observer, we too should feel that there is a touch of mystery about her. There are several movements in the course of the book; there is a maturing in Fanny and a maturing of our understanding of Fanny. She grows up and develops. She finds what she is capable of. And we too find what she is capable of.

'Is she prudish?' We might add, 'Is Jane Austen prudish?' If all Fanny's and Edmund's views were those of their creator, the answer would have to be 'yes', or at minimum, 'yes, sometimes'. But it is freely recognized that *Emma* at least is written very subjectively, and so it should be no surprise if subjectivity is found in the novel written immediately before *Emma*. Most of the action of *Mansfield Park* is seen through Fanny's eyes—in the jargon of modern criticism, she is the focalizer—and where there is stiffness, timidity, or primness of moral judgement, explicit or implied, we may suppose that it is Fanny's consciousness which is expressed rather than the author's. Yes, there is indeed primness in Fanny; the question will be whether there is anything more to her. By contrast, we are charmed by Henry and Mary. But they too are charmed by virtue. And if we feel with them, as so many readers do, we ought to join with them in seeing not only the merit of Fanny but her attractiveness.

Especially in the first half of the book, Fanny is a tender portrait of a damaged personality. She is 'delicate and puny' as a child, small for her age, and she spends a good deal of the novel in a state of uncertain health and something close to depression. In a book which studies lovelessness, she is for a long time among the unloved. The poor relation, unwanted, unvalued, she has paradoxically much in common with Mrs Norris. She could never become the vicious creature that Mrs Norris is—she has too much goodness of character, and too little energy—but her life threatens to become as bleak

115

and frustrated. She is in danger, not perhaps of being warped, but of being stunted. She notices the meagreness and cheerlessness of her aunt Norris's small house[25]—there is no indication that anyone else does so—and reproaches herself for want of attention to her; one wonders if there may be some fellow feeling in that. Her own love, in the book's earlier stages, is directed first to her brother William, who is indefinitely absent from her life, and secondarily to Edmund; tellingly not to her parents, who have in effect deserted her. She is convinced that she is unattractive, she distrusts her own judgement, and is sure that she is of no use or significance to anyone. She is a study, acutely and truthfully observed, of both emotional starvation and what modern jargon calls low self-esteem.

The damage is shown in the way that a naturally affectionate temperament has its outlets blocked. She has Edmund, and the book will study very finely how childish gratitude and affection develop into physical desire; but apart from him and, until its death, her dear old grey pony, she has nothing to love but things. 'I love this house and everything in it,' she cries, very early in the book, but let us notice the context. She is threatened with removal to Mrs Norris's dreadful tutelage, and what she clings to is a building and its contents. And what she adds a little later reveals how the love of place is a substitute for any better way of loving or feeling loved: 'If I could suppose my aunt really to care for me, it would be delightful to feel myself of consequence to any body!—*Here*, I know I am of none, and yet I love the place so well.'[29] This is a poignant study of a small wounded spirit. The potency of the house, which is almost an actor in the drama, is announced thus early. There are critics who believe that the house represents some sort of ideal for Jane Austen, but I think that it should rather appear, already, as an insidious power. The comfort that the house gives Fanny resembles the comfort that she gets from sitting with Lady Bertram: these things are like a few scraps thrown to a starveling.

'Pictures of perfection as you know make me sick and wicked,' Jane Austen once wrote in a letter to her niece Fanny Knight.[30] Again, we need to bear the context in mind: this was the conspiratorial mock-naughtiness of a favourite aunt writing to a child. Nonetheless, we might wonder if Jane Austen really intended any of her heroines to represent the perfection of virtue. Actually, Fanny Price is far less priggish than many of the heroes and heroines in contemporary novels. The heroine of Maria Edgeworth's *Belinda* breaks off her engagement to a kind and virtuous young man on the eve of her wedding and dismisses him from her life for ever because he has been gambling—this with the author's evident approval. Edgar Mandelbrote, the hero of Fanny Burney's *Camilla*, is so morally elevated that he requires his future wife to be equally flawless and casts her off without a qualm any time that there is the merest suspicion that she is less than absolutely perfect—and yet we are supposed to consider him almost a paragon, rather than a monster of cruelty and conceit. Compared with characters like these, Fanny Price is racy. And indeed she has plenty of ordinary emotions, in the way that the heroines of eighteenth- and nineteenth-century fiction too seldom do. She loves dancing. She would love to go to the theatre. She is entertained by things, even when she feels she ought not to be (significantly, this distinguishes her from Edmund, who is naturally

117

solemn and a good deal more easily shocked). She cannot help laughing when Tom Bertram makes fun of the unconscious Dr Grant, she is 'not unamused' by the bickering over the play, and despite her antagonism towards Mary Crawford, she even gets some amusement from her satiric conversation.[31]

And indeed we see small, everyday faults in her quite often—we see her angry, envious, discontented (though we also see her conscious of her own faultiness, and struggling against it). She is indeed virtuous, but hers is the virtue that comes from being subject, as most of us are, to ordinary, commonplace temptations, not that species of virtue—so much commoner in fiction than in life—which does not know what temptation is. At the ball, she feels that it is barbarous in herself to be happy while Edmund is suffering, but she knows that she derives a portion of her happiness from the very conviction that he does suffer.[32] She is allowed a bit of natural vanity, and Jane Austen's tolerance does not think that a bad thing: before the ball, she realizes that she looks good, and she looks all the better for that awareness.[33] When she refuses Henry Crawford, she supposes that he will not go on loving her, but with an expectation—perhaps a hope?—that he will not be cured too soon. For the first time she has had a triumph and holds some power over another person, and in celebration of this Jane Austen relaxes the earnestness of tone that prevails in *Mansfield Park* to enjoy Fanny's success and to tease her in the facetious manner of *Northanger Abbey*: 'How much time she might, in her own fancy, allot for its dominion, is another concern. It would not be fair to enquire into a young lady's exact estimate of her own perfections.'[34]

Fanny's detractors accuse her of being fastidious and snobbish when she returns to her family at Portsmouth. But is it not curious that the very people who condemn Fanny for being a prig or a plaster saint should blame her also for being humanly and fallibly normal? If we ask why she reacts with distress and misery to the noise and discomfort of the Portsmouth house, the essential answer is very simple: because that is how she is bound to react. Shy, physically not strong, inured to the seducing comforts of life at Mansfield Park, how could she do otherwise? We meet here an example of the exceptional truthfulness and lifelikeness of this book. To take another example of this honesty, when Fanny first sees her beloved brother William after many years' separation, she is disappointed because he is different from the William she last saw.[35] We were not expecting that, but once we hear it, we know that it is exactly right. When Fanny encounters Henry Crawford at Portsmouth, she is terrified that he will accept her father's invitation to dine at their home and discover its noisy squalor. Rationally, she should welcome anything that puts him off his unwelcome courtship of her, but the primitive shame overwhelms rational calculation.[36] The censorious critics who condemn Fanny for this, and for hating life with her own family, are themselves the prigs. It is pretty well known that teenagers are liable to find their parents embarrassing at the best of times; and these are far from the best of times. Jane Austen has the understanding to know and the truthfulness to show that this is the only possible way for Fanny to feel.

Indeed, her instinct for Fanny's feelings seems to me almost infallible. Here are two more examples. When Sir Thomas comes up to the schoolroom to press her to accept

Henry, 'The terror of his former occasional visits to that room seemed all renewed, and she felt as if he were going to examine her again in French and English.'[37] This reversion to childhood fears just as she is growing up is touching, slightly comic, and wholly believable. Or consider the joy she feels when she is called back from Portsmouth to Mansfield: it surges up, irrepressible. 'She was, she felt she was, in the greatest danger of being exquisitely happy while so many were miserable. The evil which brought such good to her! She dreaded lest she should learn to be insensible of it.'[38] Jane Austen's subjective style conveys the tumult of Fanny's emotions. The choked phrase, 'She was, she felt she was . . .' expresses the confusion of a mind that hardly knows what it feels. But at all events, if the author had designed Fanny for a plaster saint she would not have written that. Jane Austen in her picture of Fanny understands the complexity of human motive, the inextricable blend of altruism and self-gratification. Back at Mansfield, she wants to be useful, she gets satisfaction from being useful: this is the genuine outgiving of kindness and gratitude, but it also grows out of the unhappiness of others. It is part of Fanny's paradoxical achievement, her rise to influence and power.

I am disappointed by those who sneer at Fanny's misery in Portsmouth: the proper response is to sympathize with a life that has been so warped from its natural course that homecoming is turned into exile. But I am even more surprised at critics who miss the irony and subjectivity in Jane Austen's picture of Fanny's joy and suppose that she is setting up Mansfield Park as the exemplar of virtuous order and decorum. It is one example of the distortions caused by presenting Jane Austen as a conservative ideologue. ('The

Great Good Place' is a phrase applied to the Park even by Lionel Trilling, in a subtle analysis of the novel.[39]) We should remember why Sir Thomas has dispatched Fanny to Portsmouth. He intends her to become 'heartily sick' of her parents' home; his hope is that 'a little abstinence from the elegancies and luxuries of Mansfield Park, would bring her mind into a sober state' and persuade her to accept Henry Crawford.[40] What is he doing, after all—from the best motives, according to his lights—but attempting to corrupt her with the allurements of ease? How can it be supposed that in this of all novels the heroine's return from her nearest family to 'elegancies and luxuries' can represent a sort of moral progress, a triumph over temptation?

Those critics who see Fanny as an exemplar of Christian meekness and those who—perhaps making the same judgement from a different standpoint—find her a priggish milksop share the further mistake of supposing that her personality is fixed throughout the story. But part of the beauty of *Mansfield Park* is the way in which Fanny develops while remaining passive. The book has some of the elements of the *Bildungsroman*, the novel of personal development. I have reproached Virginia Woolf for saying that Jane Austen is the hardest of great writers to catch in the act of greatness, but in *Mansfield Park* there is indeed one act of greatness that is almost impossible to 'catch', or at least to demonstrate in critical prose. The development of Fanny herself and of her feelings for Edmund is so gradually and seamlessly realized that it resists illustration. Jane Austen has taken the risk of presenting her heroine as a timid, depressed child, but that is not a picture which can be sustained for ever. Maria and Julia leave Mansfield Park for a while, and the loss of their overshadowing presence allows Fanny to begin to bloom a little—quite naturally. As she becomes nubile, she becomes an object of more attraction and interest, naturally. Sir Thomas notices it and puts on a ball for her: she discovers that she can have fun and that she can look good. William's arrival unseals the fountain, and allows free expression to the natural affections that have been locked and frozen within her. And that shows to Henry Crawford that she is capable of passion.

Maybe we ourselves, the readers, have not properly realized that before. But Fanny is the most romantic of the heroines. There are transparencies of Tintern Abbey, a cave in Italy, and a lake in Cumberland on the window of the schoolroom: as Fanny, the prisoner of Mansfield Park, looks out on to the grounds which form more or less the limits of her world, she is also looking beyond, at rocks, ruins, mountains, and lands of distant romance.[41] Unlike anyone else in the house she is eager to hear about the West Indies, and she is found reading Lord Macartney's memoirs of China. 'I love to hear my uncle talk of the West Indies. I could listen to him for an hour together.'[42] We know that Sir Thomas is not a lively talker: it must be the subject, not the speaker, that allures his niece. Marianne in *Sense and Sensibility*, despite her romantic ardours, was uninterested in Colonel Brandon's experiences of the South Seas: Fanny is alone among the heroines in her curiosity about the exotic. She would be stage-struck, if only she had the opportunity: she wishes she could see a play, but has never had the chance; even Henry reading Shakespeare is exciting to her.[43] (It is false to say, as is often said, that she has a puritan objection to plays altogether. On the contrary, her objection to the play-acting at the Park has an element of renunciation in it: indeed, Henry's acting 'had first taught Fanny what the pleasure of a play might be'.)

She enjoys nature and landscape: on the journey to Sotherton, her first, brief escape from Mansfield, she is looking about her at the soil, the cottages, the cattle, the children; in this she is contrasted with Mary, who has small interest in 'nature, inanimate nature': 'her attention was all for men and women' (like Lizzy Bennet, or Jane Austen, for that matter).[44] Fanny loves the antiquity of Sotherton and the patina of historical association around it; she is disappointed by the modernity of the chapel. She recoils from the enthusiasm for remodelling old houses, rampant in Mr Rushworth and Henry Crawford. She finds medievalizing romance in Edmund Bertram's Christian name—'It is a name of heroism and renown—of kings, princes, and knights; and seems to breathe the spirit of chivalry and warm affections'—while thoroughly modern Mary likes the sound of 'Mr Bertram'.[45] (For Fanny 'Mr Bertram' is 'so cold and nothing-meaning . . . It just stands for a gentleman, and that's all.' We might notice how inadequate the idea of gentlemanliness is for this heroine.) A starlit night prompts her to a rhapsody on the 'sublimity of Nature'; such beauty must leave all music, art, and poetry far behind, she declares, and 'lift the heart to rapture'. The world would be happier and better, if 'people were carried more out of themselves by contemplating such a scene'.[46] What she wants is ecstasy, in the strict sense of the word; and no other of the heroines speaks like this, not even Marianne. But she is indoors as she utters these words, looking through the window at the stars, just as she must look through the window to see the representations of Tintern and Italy. Edmund invites her out on to the lawn to see more constellations, and she quickly agrees, but he then postpones and forgets the pleasure, moving to join a group of singers gathered round the instrument. It is a small victory of the house over the open space beyond, of polite society over romance, of Mary over Fanny, of culture over nature. But it is not a final victory.

Mansfield Park tells how Fanny wins Edmund Bertram, but it is also a story of her achieving a kind of independence of him. It is a story of binding and of liberation. There is a scene early in the book where Edmund invites Fanny to discuss the Crawfords with him.[47] It is a passage which turned Kingsley Amis purple:

> But it is not long before Edmund is shocked by Mary Crawford's complaint—in company too—that her uncle's rather ill-judged alterations to a cottage of his resulted in the garden being messed up for some time. Soon afterwards he conducts, with the untiringly sycophantic Fanny, a post-mortem on this affront to his 'sense of propriety'. This readiness to be shocked [is] in itself shocking ...

It seems worth quoting this attack (which gets even fiercer—'canting pietistic tirade'), because Amis has seen something important and yet missed the point entirely. The point is that Edmund does not really want to explore the question of the Crawfords with Fanny: he wants a sounding board. At the end of the scene, Jane Austen sums up: 'Having formed her mind and gained her affections, he had a good chance of her thinking like him; ...' Here the author uses the technique, so well employed in *Pride and Prejudice*, of letting the characters reveal themselves in dialogue before giving her own explanation of them. At moments Edmund has almost catechized his cousin: 'But was there nothing in her conversation that struck you Fanny, as not quite right?' And then, upon her replying, he says, 'I thought you would be struck.' He brings the scene to an end with the words, 'I am glad you saw it all as I did.'

So a delicate irony plays over a scene which Amis and many other readers have taken unironically. But the irony goes further. For Fanny did not quite see it all as he did: she dissents, to some degree, from his view of Mary. But Edmund has merely wanted to hear his own judgements confirmed, and he has not been listening. He is also beginning, already, to deceive himself. There is in Miss Crawford, he says, 'nothing sharp, or loud, or coarse', and we have already seen, in the chapter before, where Mary makes a startlingly coarse joke, that this is not entirely true. I have already quoted part of Jane Austen's sentence summing up the scene; let me now complete it: '. . . he had a good chance of her thinking like him; though at this period, and on this subject, there began now to be some danger of dissimilarity for he was in a line of admiration of Miss Crawford.' For the most part we have heard Fanny indeed parroting the views of the man who has 'formed her mind', but we have just marked the first hints of disagreement, and increasingly her judgements of people will stand independently from his (though of course they will remain at one on fundamental matters of religion and moral principle).

It seems strange to me that so many critics should suppose Jane Austen, the subtlest ironist in English fiction, to have been unaware that Edmund is a bit of a prig. She knows very well what she is doing. When Mary talks humorously about the improvements to his garden made by her guardian,

125

referred to with light satire as 'my honoured uncle', the reaction is this: 'Edmund was sorry to hear Miss Crawford, whom he was much disposed to admire, speak so freely of her uncle. It did not suit his sense of propriety . . .'[48] But Mary's words were enjoyable and quite harmless, and indeed rather like some of Jane Austen's own letters; Fanny, for her part, has shown interest in the subject. Edmund is indeed too stuffy. Only a little later comes Mary's joke about buggery. Such grossness appears so improbable in Miss Austen's chaste pages, above all on the lips of a lady, that one may wonder if one has misunderstood, but the purport seems inescapable: ' "Certainly, my home at my uncle's brought me acquainted with a circle of admirals. Of *Rears*, and *Vices*, I saw enough. Now, do not be suspecting me of a pun, I entreat." '[49] Such a joke is a surprise in itself; but it is a further surprise— and significant—that Jane Austen chooses this of all moments to show up not Mary but Edmund: 'Edmund again felt grave, and only replied, "It is a noble profession." ' It is a dull reader who does not feel this to be comic. We would expect the moralist to give the goody a small victory in this place, but Jane Austen allows Mary to 'win'. She is content to make gentle fun of Edmund, as she was of Edward Ferrars, another honourable, dull young man who is preparing to enter the Church. It is a sign of her daring and freedom. Later, when plans for the theatricals are being laid, Edmund observes that it must be difficult to keep the clergyman Anhalt—the character whom he will eventually agree to play—'from appearing a formal, solemn lecturer'.[50] There is something a little touching about this—as though Edmund half recognizes a flaw in himself. The author herself also seems to be self-referential here: for her too it will be difficult to avoid representing Edmund as a solemn stick. She adver-tises the risk that she is taking.

We need to distinguish priggishness from firmness of moral judgement. In the cases of Mary and Henry, Fanny judges more hardly than Edmund does, but I do not think that she is unreasonably censorious: her criticisms of them are tough, but just and accurate. She has seen the elements of corruption in them which others have not seen, and she puts her finger on the spot. Her doubts about Mary begin before the time when she has cause to be jealous of her, and she is allowed to feel Mary's charm, and in part succumb to it. Though jealousy plays a part in the complex mixture of feel-ings that Fanny comes to have towards Mary, it does not importantly warp her judgement.

Fanny seems most priggish when she is seconding Edmund—in the discussion that he initiates about the Craw-fords, and in opposing the play. I do not want to get drawn far into the complex issues surrounding the play, but again I am surprised that so many people assume that the attitudes of Edmund and Fanny to it are straightforwardly Jane Austen's own. Here too she makes things difficult for herself. *Lovers' Vows*, Mrs Inchbald's adaptation of a play by Kotzebue, far from being subversive of morality, is almost ludicrously goody-goody: the adapter had indeed altered the German original to ensure that it should be so. (The play is also extraordinarily bad: the only thing of any merit in it is the comic butler, who seems to have strayed in from another play—indeed his farcically inept verses, preposterously at variance with the rest of the drama, were supplied to the authoress by a collaborator.) It never occurs to the older persons in the house, Lady Bertram and Mrs Norris, that there is any impropriety in these amateur dramatics, and though neither of these women is a good judge, their attitude does at least suggest that the play-acting is not blatantly wrong or unconventional. In the argument between Tom and Edmund, the former pressing for the play, the latter urging that the idea should be abandoned, the honours are about even; certainly Tom is not made to lose. With his disarming good humour in laughing at himself for using a bad argument (he has suggested that Lady Bertram needs cheering up at a time of anxiety about her husband, and then shot a glance at her torpid placidity) Tom may well seem the more engaging of the two disputants. Similarly, when Sir Thomas returns unexpectedly, Tom's amusement at Yates's instant transformation from the passionate Baron Wildenheim to a polite young man seems to win the reader's sympathy and collaboration.[51]

Edmund has a mild unease about private theatricals in general and a strong objection to them in the present circumstances.[52] His first objection is that it shows lack of feeling for the absent Sir Thomas. This is an argument which may have carried more weight among Jane Austen's first readers than it is likely to do today, but we have already had reason to suspect that Edmund's deference to his seniors may be excessive, and the action of the story will go on to show the disastrousness of repressing the natural spirits of the young. It is not obvious that this argument should be regarded as strong. Edmund's second argument is closer to the heart of the matter: it would be imprudent with regard to Maria, 'whose situation is a very delicate one, considering every thing, very delicate'. It is perhaps not clear how much Edmund has realized—certainly no one suspects how great the catastrophe will be at last—but there is a right instinct at work here. What Jane Austen seems to have portrayed, with psychological acuity, is a moral unease that cannot quite justify itself. Her own experience of amateur dramatics is revealed in the beautifully observed depiction of the bickerings and petty vanities that spring up among the actors— comedy in the familiar Austen style.

Fanny, for her part, is indeed shocked by *Lovers' Vows*: 'Agatha and Amelia appeared to her in their different ways so totally improper for home representation—the situation of one, and the language of the other, so unfit to be expressed by any woman of modesty . . .'[53] That does strike us as priggish. How did Miss Austen feel? We do not precisely know the answer to that, nor do we need to know. Jane Austen represents Fanny thus, because it is how, at this stage in her development, she is bound to feel. But this is not the only Fanny whom we shall see. Later in the book, after Henry's proposal, she will burst out with what is perhaps the most feminist statement in the whole canon, protesting against the presumption that a 'generally agreeable' man may reasonably expect reciprocal affection from the woman on whom he bestows his love.[54] Is this Fanny? Yet this distressed and passionate outburst grows entirely convincingly out of her character and situation. Later still, when she gets a letter from Edmund, its contents irritate her; she is tempted to think Sir Thomas unkind, she feels bitterly towards Mary, and she is 'almost vexed into displeasure, and anger, against Edmund'—actually, rather thoroughly vexed and angry with him, we may reckon, once we learn the content of her thoughts.[55] These may be imperfectly Christian sentiments, but the reader is likely to feel a kind of satisfaction that Fanny has at last acquired the spunkiness to express to herself such forceful indignation and scorn. It is a last stage of her development towards an adult independence and fullness of emotion.

The plenitude of her satisfaction spills out beyond the end of the book. On the last page we learn that Edmund acquires the Mansfield living 'just after they had been married long enough to begin to want an increase of income'. In a majority of cases Jane Austen does not so much as hint at the heroine's pregnancy. (Marianne is described as becoming 'the mistress of a family', in a context which does not unambiguously indicate children, and Emma contemplates the prospect of her nephew losing the chance to inherit Donwell Abbey.) At first blush we might think it surprising that the author does not include children as part of that felicity to which she dismisses her heroines. But on reflection we might rather admire her refined sense of closure—her feeling for the demands of form and for the story's proper limits. In other novelists who present us with a flock of children at the end of their books we may feel a kind of looseness, an emotional indulgence which is aesthetically not quite satisfying. Of the six novels *Pride and Prejudice* is the one most like this: we are informed what happened to Mr Bennet, to Wickham and Lydia, and so on. This is less sophisticated than the endings of the later books, perhaps, but still it represents a tying up of the ends of the old story. The birth of children, by contrast, is the start of something new. But in Fanny's case there is just a hint of the motherhood to come, and that is fitting, because her story, unlike that of the other heroines, is not of a few months' duration only: we see her earlier and follow her a little further.

Jane Austen has wanted to depict a heroine who is good and gentle but (if only a little) damaged. It is a very difficult portrayal to bring off. Dickens tried in *Little Dorrit* to depict a heroine who was essentially pure and virtuous and yet somehow touched with the taint of her upbringing in a debtors' prison, but he, who could do some things better than any novelist who has ever lived, could not manage this. Amy Dorrit's alleged taint remains a datum, asserted by the author, but not adequately realized in the story. However, Jane Austen does, I believe, succeed with Fanny. There is something desolating about Fanny's pleasure at her return from her natural family's vivid, noisy, slatternly life in Portsmouth, where she has been able to see her adored brother William after a long separation, to the barren comforts of Mansfield Park. To sit in the drawing room for hours by Lady Bertram, whose noblest passion is a faint good nature, is a relief! Fanny has been growing up at Portsmouth, but her wings have been clipped.

The moral poise of the Portsmouth episode is very delicate. In a *Bildungsroman* we expect any particular stage in the hero's experience to develop his maturity and understanding (or alternatively to give him a push on the downward slope). With Fanny at Portsmouth Jane Austen's wisdom is to show a more complex process: Fanny goes both forwards and back. Her life is both freer and more restricted. She is cramped in the Prices' narrow, noisy house, yet she enjoys more personal independence than she has had before. We see her weakness in the difficulty that she finds in coping with her new circumstances, but at the same time she is growing in a generous recognition of her weakness. She becomes able to see through the rough manners of her sister Susan to realize that Susan is in an important respect better than herself: Susan is trying to be useful and set things to rights, whereas Fanny (as she tells herself) would only have gone away and cried. But meanwhile Fanny is learning the pleasures of patronage and modest freedom: she can settle a children's squabble by buying Betsey her knife, teach Susan the rudiments of refinement, join a library and choose her own books. As with the schoolroom at Mansfield, she annexes a space and makes it her own, in this case the upstairs room which becomes a retreat for Susan and herself. By a touching irony, the very lack of a fire here reminds her of the Mansfield schoolroom, that space of such emotional importance. Fanny becomes Susan's 'oracle'; the pleasure of genuine, unselfish kindness and the more self-assertive pleasures of patronage are intertwined.

Fanny's territory expands, physically and emotionally, in the course of the story; the power of place is an idea that pervades the book, and this expansion is an instance of it. At first her room is a garret, the 'little white attic' allotted to her as the poor relation who must be taught to understand the limited future that lies before her.[56] But gradually she colonizes the schoolroom, and it becomes accepted that it is her place. When Sir Thomas directs that a fire shall be lit in the room, it becomes comfortable; this is Fanny's first small victory over Mrs Norris (who had decreed the absence of a fire), presaging the lady's later and more complete defeat. Once superfluous, Fanny becomes essential: after the disaster of Maria's elopement, when she has been brought back from Portsmouth, she becomes necessary to the emotional stability of the house. She in effect fixes Lady Bertram's future, and engineers her own escape from Lady

Bertram, by providing her sister Susan as a substitute in the role of dutiful attendant. When she marries Edmund, she goes off to Thornton Lacey, but in the book's last sentences, she returns with him to the parsonage at Mansfield. It would be too much to say that she becomes the mistress of Mansfield (Tom will presumably marry in due course, and he and his wife will reign at the Park after Sir Thomas's demise), but she is the principal functioning female on the scene at the book's close: Maria, Julia, Mary, and Mrs Norris are all gone, in varying degrees of disgrace or defeat, and Lady Bertram does not function.[57]

Henry James, perhaps unconsciously, was to borrow the fundamental idea of *Mansfield Park* in *The Golden Bowl*: each is the story of an unassuming woman who has to deal with a more vivid rival for the possession of her man, and quietly, slowly sees her off against the odds. Meek, timid Fanny Price is actually the most powerful of all the heroines—in two senses. First, she is presented as a kind of virtuous usurper. Second, the way she decides to act determines not only her own life but transforms the lives of several others. Henry Crawford, Mary Crawford, Mrs Rushworth, and Mrs Norris would all have had radically different lives if Fanny had only accepted Henry; and Sir Thomas and Lady Bertram, as well as Edmund of course, are also deeply and permanently affected by the consequences of her decision. None other of the heroines has this kind of power over the people around her. If Knightley and Emma should not marry, Highbury will carry on just the same; if Wentworth and Anne do not marry, it will compromise the happiness only of themselves. Jane Austen wants us to notice that Fanny has this power. Uniquely, she offers us an alternative ending in her final chapter, telling us that if Henry had persisted in his courtship of Fanny, he would probably have succeeded, and probably been happy; if Edmund and Mary had married, Henry's success with Fanny would have been certain.[58] 'I have been a selfish being all my life . . . By you, I was properly humbled. I came to you without a doubt of my reception. You showed me how insufficient were all my pretensions to please a woman worthy of being pleased.'[59] That of course is Darcy to Elizabeth Bennet, and if we cannot quite imagine Henry Crawford saying the same to Fanny—for whereas Darcy is proud, Henry is essentially vain—we can still see how nearly similar the two men's fates might have been. For happiness, Henry needs Fanny, and she does not need him.

If we were to hazard a guess at which protagonist in fiction was the least likely to be described as 'daemonic', Miss Price might well head the list. But so it is. After Maria's elopement, 'Mrs Norris . . . was but the more irritated by the sight of the person whom, in the blindness of her anger, she could have charged as the daemon of the piece.'[60] Mrs Norris's is of course a perverted judgement, but her premiss is correct: 'Had Fanny accepted Mr. Crawford, this could not have happened.' Mary too acknowledges the power that lay in Fanny's possession: 'She would have fixed him, she would have made him happy for ever.'[61] The subterranean plot pattern in *Mansfield Park* is that of the successful adventuress, who rises from humble beginnings to social triumph, seeing off anyone who gets in her way. It is a splendid irony, both witty and touching, that this role is handed to so gentle and self-effacing a creature. Fanny is, as it were, the good stepsister to Becky Sharp and Undine Spragg, and in the end more fully successful than either. She becomes the cuckoo who kicks the other offspring out of the nest. Edmund calls her 'my only sister now' (not of course quite what she wants to hear). For Sir Thomas she becomes 'the daughter that he wanted'.[62] The weakliest of the heroines has become the most potent.

Some critics have found it hard to believe that a lively, worldly man like Henry Crawford could ever have fallen for a good little mouse like Fanny, but on the contrary, he is exactly the type of man who marries his secretary. It is significant that he is said to be plain: he needs to prove to himself his power of conquest. Henry is vain: he wants power and he wants admiration. He knows that Fanny is pretty and gentle, but he also comes to realize that she is passionate: he has seen this from the warmth and strength of her love for her brother.[63] It is not going very far beyond the text to say that what Henry has recognized is that she is likely to be good in bed. But he also wants adoration. His sister sees it at once: 'I approve your choice from my soul, and foresee your happiness as heartily as I wish and desire it. You will have a sweet little wife; all gratitude and devotion.'[64] Here he comes closest to another Henry—Tilney, in *Northanger Abbey*. Tilney is drawn in the first place to Catherine Morland because she is partial to him; he enjoys basking in the admiration of a simple, artless girl:[65]

> ... though Henry was now sincerely attached to her, though he felt and delighted in all the excellencies of her character and truly loved her society, I must confess that his affection originated in nothing better than gratitude, or, in other words, that a persuasion of her partiality for him had been the only cause of giving her a second thought. It is a new

circumstance in romance, I acknowledge, and dreadfully derogatory of a heroine's dignity; but if it be as new in common life, the credits of a wild imagination will at least be all my own.

As Jane Austen here points out, she is simply being true to life: genuine love and affection may be inextricably bound up with a gentle vanity and the gratification of self-esteem. Of course, Henry Tilney is genuinely amiable as Henry Crawford is not, but the mainsprings of their emotions are not dissimilar. Jane Austen's art is to understand similarity and difference—to create characters who resemble one another and yet are unlike. And the irony in Henry Crawford's case is that he has misread: Fanny, who is a great deal meeker than Catherine, is not half so simple and artless: she is a tough, severe judge (and she has grown up in a grand house, after all, not like Catherine in a country rectory).

It seems very crude to divide Jane Austen's characters into the good and the bad, but in broad terms it can be done. In those terms Henry and Mary are the only 'bad' or potentially 'bad' characters in the novels who face a moral struggle and whose moral status is worked out in the action of the narrative. Wickham is a rogue disguised as a victim, Isabella Thorpe selfishness wearing the mask of friendship, William Elliot a cynical dissembler, but in each of these cases the action reveals the true nature that has existed all along. Willoughby comes nearest to the Crawfords: he is genuinely pained by his villainy, but his smoothness has seemed suspect from the start, and his character as in due course uncovered is such that there could be no serious doubt that he would put money before duty and affection. But the outcome with both Henry and Mary is genuinely in doubt. It is part of the serious, rather sombre air of *Mansfield Park* that so many of the characters are engaged in the moral wrestle. The book's spirit is summed up in Jane Austen's concluding words about 'the advantages of early hardship and discipline and the consciousness of being born to struggle and endure'.[66]

She plays cunningly with the expectations induced by the novel of manners as a genre. Henry and Mary begin as attractive but worldly people. It may be worth noticing that Mary has dark eyes, a brown complexion, and is not tall, with a light figure and nimble movement.[67] In these respects, as in her liveliness of face and wit in speech, she resembles Elizabeth Bennet; Edmund excuses her by saying, 'She does not *think* evil, but she speaks it—speaks it in playfulness'— and that last word is one especially associated with Lizzy. I think that Jane Austen may have been consciously composing a variation on a theme; with happier influences on her earlier life, and with only a slight alteration in the balance of her character, Mary might have emulated Lizzy Bennet's naughty virtue. At Mansfield Henry and Mary begin to get away from the corrupting influence of the uncle who has brought them up, and each falls in love with a good person: the movement of the story is towards virtue. It looks as though Mary and Henry will be redeemed: Henry in the presence of Fanny, Mary in her scene with Fanny in the schoolroom feel the captivations of goodness. Halfway through the book, and for some time after, the natural development of the plot would seem to be for Fanny to soften towards Henry and make a better man of him (after all, the author tells us herself that this might easily have happened), and for Mary to be improved by marriage to Edmund. For we have come to care for Henry and Mary, and this is a comedy, is it not, and what is more, a comedy with a moral tone? Surely the obvious, indeed the only way to bring about a proper ending is for Edmund to marry Mary and Fanny to marry Henry, with each of the Crawfords thus finding their salvation? The answer, of course, is that the book proves to be hardly a comedy at all. The *peripeteia* of the action sees the wreckage of the hopes, reputation, or happiness of almost all the principal characters. The heroine gets her man, but as we have seen, even this is relegated to a kind of postscript.

It is natural in a comedy of manners for the author to indicate what the denouement will be and perhaps even how it will be contrived some time before it actually occurs. That is, for example, part of the pleasure we take in the unravelment of *Pride and Prejudice.* In the Portsmouth part of *Mansfield Park* we get a number of hints of this kind, suggesting that we are moving towards a marriage between Fanny and Henry. We catch Fanny hoping that Henry will not be put off her by the vulgarity of her family (Lizzy Bennet had similar feelings).[68] We see the transformation of his manners: he is now more agreeable, attentive to the feelings of others, kind to Susan, gracious towards Fanny's vulgar father—all pretty comparable to the transformation in the manners of Mr Darcy.[69] Fanny and Henry start to find shared tastes: 'The loveliness of the day, and of the view, he felt like herself. They often stopt with the same sentiment and taste, leaning against a wall, some minutes, to look and admire.'[70] (We might think back to how captivated Fanny had been at Mansfield by the style in which Henry read Shakespeare.)[71] Lastly, Fanny daydreams about how she would be able to take Susan into her own home, were she to marry Henry: 'She thought he was really good-tempered, and could fancy his entering into a plan of that sort, most pleasantly.'[72] At this point almost nine-tenths of the book are already past, but the outcome is still uncertain. If Jane Austen had broken off here, I doubt whether we could have been confident of what the ending was to be. Contrast the method of *Pride and Prejudice*, where even the title pretty well tells us what will happen. The continuing uncertainty in *Mansfield Park* is partly a matter of narrative technique, but it is also an expression of the book's moral economy: so late in the story Henry's possibilities—ruin or redemption—still hang in the balance.

What is the natural *ethos* of Henry or of Mary? We do not exactly know the answer to that. But we do know that they have had to live in circumstances having a tendency to corrupt, and that they are, at least fitfully, aware of it themselves. Mary warns her brother that the 'contagion' of the Admiral's manners is liable to damage him, and that 'your marrying early may be the saving of you. To have seen you grow like the Admiral in word or deed, look or gesture, would have broken my heart.'[73] There are warmth, affection, and goodness in those words. But both Henry and Mary have the habit of pre-empting criticism by criticizing themselves, and softening the edge of self-examination with humour. Mary tells Fanny that she knows she has behaved extremely ill, 'and therefore, if you please, you must forgive me. Selfishness must be forgiven you know, because there is no hope of a cure.' 'Nothing ever fatigues me [she adds], but doing what I do not like. Miss Price, I give way to you with a very bad grace; . . .' Later Henry tosses off the comic aside, 'I never do wrong without gaining by it.'[74]

This style of humour, half self-deprecating, half complacent, is one of the external marks of Henry and Mary's kinship. Henry has the instincts of a hunter: Fanny's resistance stimulates in him the desire to have 'the glory, as well as the felicity, of forcing her to love him'.[75] Mary also delights in the pleasure of conquest, but with a more inward eroticism: 'His sturdy spirit to bend as it did! Oh! it was sweet beyond expression.'[76] That is from her half-soliloquy in the east room, recalling Edmund during the 'acting week' which gave her a time of exquisite happiness, she says, such as she has never known. The Crawfords have moral taste. Henry is able to feel shame at the comparison between himself and William Price.[77] His love for Fanny includes a love of her goodness and gentleness. True, he is drawn to her demureness partly through the vanity that looks for a quietly adoring wife, but also through a genuine attraction to virtue: he values her principles and her religion, we are told, and he repents of his original scheme, to hurt her a little and then let her be.[78]

The mastery of these two portraits does indeed lie to a great extent in the way that the Crawfords' virtues and vices are shown to be intertwined; their very faults are the means by which they might be saved. The great scene in the east room develops a psychological complexity in the depiction of inner struggle that had hardly been attempted in fiction before, perhaps not at all. Partly Mary is talking to herself, partly she is exercising the arts of persuasion on Fanny; partly she is pouring out her love for Fanny and Fanny's gentle virtue, and partly trying to manipulate her; partly putting on the mask and partly opening up, with a new frankness, her inner emptiness, and a sense of loss or lack.

Our response as readers is likely to be complex too: partly we shall deplore Mary's continued worldliness and calculation, partly we should be moved. Her love for Edmund, her memory of brief exquisite happiness is very poignant, though it is intermingled—for there is a doubleness in Mary here also—with that pleasure in subduing Edmund's spirit which is not only an expression of *eros* but also a will to moral hurt; for she purposes to turn him from his vocation as a clergyman. Other than the heroines, she is perhaps the only character in the novels whose mental life is opened up to us in this way.

These pages would deserve detailed analysis, sentence by sentence, but for the moment I shall make do with just one of Mary's speeches:[79]

Yes, very true. Mrs. Fraser has been my intimate friend for years. But I have not the least inclination to go near her. I can think only of the friends I am leaving; my excellent sister, yourself, and the Bertrams in general. You have all so much more *heart* among you, than one finds in the world at large. You all give me a feeling of being able to trust and confide in you; which, in common intercourse, one knows nothing of. I wish I had settled with Mrs. Fraser not to go to her till after Easter, a much better time for the visit—but now I cannot put her off. And when I have done with her, I must go to her sister, Lady Stornoway, because *she* was rather my most particular friend of the two; but I have not cared much for *her* these three years.

The beginning and end of this are the ordinary rattle of conventional worldliness, with its utterly superficial notion of what friendship means. But in between Mary shows an awareness of the moral dimension of friendship. The context means that this moral dimension is perceived in a peculiar way: Mary values the niceness of Mrs Grant, Fanny, and Sir Thomas because she finds it more comfortable: it is simply more agreeable to be among decent, good-hearted people than out in the cold wide world. Yet hers is a moral feeling, nonetheless. The Crawfords will need to be persuaded of the attractiveness of virtue if they are to embrace it (that is why Mary does not want Edmund to be ordained: because a clergyman is such a dreary thing to be). But perhaps an appreciation of charm may be one of the paths to salvation.

We have already seen something of the significance of place in *Mansfield Park*. 'I know Mansfield, I know its way, I know its faults towards *you*,' Henry tells Fanny.[80] His use of the place to stand for the people is a *façon de parler*, but telling nonetheless. For not only the sense of place but the power of place is pervasive in this book. This is the only time that Jane Austen named a novel after a place (*Northanger Abbey* is a posthumous title, chosen by Jane's brother Henry—the earlier version, accepted for publication but never brought out, was called *Susan*); otherwise, the novels are named from people or their characteristics. It is also significant that the book is named not just from a place but from a house. In *Emma* the presence and character of the large village of Highbury become important, and in *Sanditon* (again not Jane Austen's choice of name, though it seems suitable enough) she seems to have been trying the experiment of making the town and its development almost a character in the story; but the village of Mansfield is barely visible. We hear of a few cottages. The reference to Fanny's 'works of charity and ingenuity' to be seen in the schoolroom, and the statement that before her visit to Portsmouth she had been 'wholly unused to confer favours, except on the very poor',[81] are momentary indications of the humble existences beyond the Park's gates: Fanny must have done a little of that visiting of the poor that is seen more explicitly in Emma Woodhouse and Anne Elliot. There are evidently no gentry or half-gentry in Mansfield village apart from the parson and his wife and Mrs Norris in her cottage; it may be very small, and it seems to be conceived as an estate village, its economy dependent on the Park. The book's very last sentence, with its reference to Fanny's love for everything 'within the view and patronage of Mansfield Park', is again telling. The Park has power, the view is outward from the Park; and once more the Park is personified.

Classic drama supposedly observed the unities, including the unity of place: all the action of the play (so the theorists said) should happen on the same spot of earth. No novel is likely to be as immobile as that, but in *Mansfield Park*, and again in *Emma*, Jane Austen makes meaning out of the inter-play between observing and breaching the principle of unity of place. This is a new development in her art: in the earlier novels the young women move around the country when it suits the plot for them to do so, and without their movements being freighted with a weight of meaning. But in both *Mansfield Park* and *Emma* the heroine is fixed in one place for most of the duration of the action, and when she does move from that fixed spot, the movement has a peculiar signifi-cance. Fanny's story begins with her being brought to Mansfield Park from afar, and there she is held, as unable to move from the place physically as she is unable to spread her wings metaphorically. The trip to Sotherton is a great event for her: although it is only ten miles from Mansfield, Fanny is 'soon beyond her knowledge'. Some time later it is still quite an affair for her to dine with three other people half a mile from home, 'for excepting the day at Sotherton, she had scarcely ever dined out before'.[82] She has never been to Thornton Lacey, Edmund's future living, though it is only eight miles away.[83] We learn, as it were casually, late in the book that one of her sisters at Portsmouth has died in her absence, but there was evidently no question of her leaving Mansfield either before or after the death. William is able to visit her at Mansfield, but there is no possibility that she might come to him. When she finally does leave Mansfield, the change of scene carries much moral importance. It is a transformation scene: like Cinderella at the stroke of midnight, Fanny is whisked abruptly from luxury to poverty. But it also transforms Fanny herself.

The bright mobility of the Crawfords, flitting rapidly to and from Mansfield, contrasts with Fanny's fixity. But it is not only Fanny who is subject to Mansfield Park's constraining power: there is a family contrast between the Crawfords and the Bertrams as a whole. Maria and Julia too are held in thrall by the Park. The Bertrams used to have a house in town, but Sir Thomas has given it up: the boundaries around his daughters have been tightened.[84] A house in town becomes Maria's 'prime object', one of the baits that lure her into accepting Rushworth.[85] This is how Jane Austen describes her state of mind after Henry Crawford jilts her:[86]

> He [Henry] should not have to think of her as pining in the retirement of Mansfield for *him*, rejecting Sotherton and London, independence and splendour for *his* sake. Independence was more needful than ever; the want of it at

Mansfield more sensibly felt. She was less and less able to endure the restraint which her father imposed. The liberty which his absence had given was now become absolutely necessary. She must escape from him and Mansfield as soon as possible, . . .

The language is telling, the subterraneous metaphor of imprisonment sustained: restraint, liberty, escape. It is telling too that the proper nouns are all places: Sotherton, London, and Mansfield, Mansfield, Mansfield. To be sure, this is partly an indication of Maria's character: her lust is for external comforts and pleasures; she thinks about Mr Rushworth's house, while Mr Rushworth's person has faded from her view. But Jane Austen's language also expresses a feeling for the significance of places as areas which one may possess with the power of enjoyment, or which conversely exercise power upon oneself.

Her exploration of the significance of place and area is most strikingly visible in the visit to Sotherton, where she makes her experiment with what one is bound to call symbolism. The lawn enclosed by a wall, Mary Crawford wanting to pass beyond the door in the wall and finding it unlocked, her leading the way into the 'wilderness' beyond and talking with Edmund there (and making an explicit comparison with the metaphorical 'wilderness' of a lawyer's profession)—the symbolic force of these things needs no explication.[87] Christ was tempted in the wilderness, as were the Israelites before him, and Mary acts the temptress's part, pressing Edmund to abandon his plan to become a clergyman. In the next chapter the symbolism is plainer still. Henry tells Maria that she has 'a very smiling scene' before her. 'Do you mean literally or figuratively?' Maria replies, preparing us for the fusion of literal and figurative in the episode that follows. Maria continues, 'Yes, certainly the sun shines and the park looks very cheerful. But unluckily that iron gate, that ha-ha, give me a feeling of restraint and hardship. I cannot get out, as the starling said.' Rushworth has the key, and is slow in bringing it. Henry questions whether she needs Rushworth's authority and protection, and suggests that with his own help she could get round the edge of the gate and allow herself 'to think it not prohibited'. Fanny anxiously warns her that she will hurt herself on the spikes, tear her gown, and may slip into the ha-ha.[88]

Some critics have been particularly drawn to this episode (rather like those musicologists who are happiest with Mozart when he can seem to be anticipating Beethoven). Others seem to be uncomfortable with it: perhaps they think that the allegory sits awkwardly in a naturalistic novel, or perhaps they feel that the foreshadowing of Maria's adultery and self-destruction is too *voulu*. I believe that it works well, partly because the figurative and the literal are so nearly and naturally fused. For the women in the story, the places in which they live, and their ability or inability to get away from them, are issues of prime emotional importance. Sotherton and Mr Rushworth can only be had as part of a single package—that indeed is Maria's problem. And in the question whether she can 'get out' the literal and figurative elements are hardly to be separated: her elopement with Henry will be a flight both from the emotional emptiness of her marriage and from the physical constraint which requires a wife to be where her husband is. The symbolism works also because Henry is fully conscious of it, and Maria is at least partly so. It is not imposed from the outside, but developed by the characters themselves: it is part of Henry's apparatus of flirtation, his testing of Maria to see how far she might go. He will treat the play in the same way, well aware of the relationships between the parts taken by the actors and their own feelings. (Here, however, the irony is more complex, because the parts do not 'fit'. As Frederick, Henry can address Maria, playing Agatha, in accents of passion, and she him, but it is the wrong kind of passion. Frederick is Agatha's son. Agatha is, as Maria will become, a fallen woman; but Henry will be no more prepared to marry Maria than Frederick would be to marry his mother.)

Within Mansfield Park itself Jane Austen finds a sense of the significance of interior space—of what might be called moral space. This sense can be related to something else that she first discovers in this novel: the poignancy of objects. She understands the tenderness of personal ownership, especially in childhood or early youth. At Portsmouth we see Susan and Betsey battling for the possession of a little silver knife, and Betsey's satisfaction at owning the knife which Fanny buys her to mend the quarrel. In *Emma* Harriet's relics of Mr Elton—a piece of court-plaster and the stub of a pencil—are reverently labelled '*Most precious treasures*', and like the heroine herself, we hardly know whether to laugh or cry.[89] A similar poignancy attaches to the spaces which the child Fanny 'owns'. These spaces are intensely realized, yet with almost no description. Concerning the attic in which Fanny begins we know only that it is small and white and that there is no fire.[90] But this cold, pure, pale place is vivid to us as part of our understanding of Fanny. What we know of the old schoolroom is that it faces east and that it is chilly until Sir Thomas's intervention (since Mrs Norris has forbidden a fire to be lit there);[91] the transparencies of picturesque views are on the window, and it is where Fanny keeps a few of her particular treasures. It has become Fanny's space, and it is imbued with her moral presence. It is here that the great scene takes place in which Mary Crawford comes to press her to marry Henry. Mary is moved by the room as soon as she enters it. 'The east room. Only once was I in this room before! . . . Only once before.' Of course her emotion springs from the memory of Edmund. But it is significant that she has felt the power of place, and that it is strong enough to divert her from her purpose: she is turned aside 'by the sudden change in Miss Crawford's ideas; by the strong effect on her mind which the finding herself in the east room again produced.' She visits, as a pilgrim, the place of past happiness: we see her 'stopping to look about her, and seemingly to retrace all that then had passed'. 'Here we were, just in this part of the room; here was your cousin, here was I, here were the chairs.—Oh! Why will such things ever pass away?' She measures the coordinates in space, here, and here, and here.[92]

But the room is Fanny's moral space rather than Edmund's, and Mary experiences a second diversion of her emotions. She finds the pleasure of loving the whole family of the beloved: 'Nay, in sober sadness, I believe I now love you all.' And she finds herself especially loving Fanny, embracing her where she had meant to scold her, and as she hangs upon the weeping girl, she laments that she is about to lose being in the company of gentleness and amiability as she leaves Mansfield to plunge into the glitter of the world. The psychology of Mary's wrestle in this scene between her good and ill impulses is very subtle. By the end, she has recovered her poise and her speech has become calculated once more, but in the meantime she has learnt how place, space, and memory may stir the emotions, and even act as the advocates of moral reformation.

5

The Prisoner of Hartfield

In giving so much importance to the settings of *Mansfield Park* and *Emma* Jane Austen was moving on to new ground: she had provided very little background in *Pride and Prejudice*, a novel in which place is unimportant. This is one more instance of that book's theatrical character, for in a stage work there can be no elaborated background: the playwright can present only what the characters say and do, and the furniture or scenery immediately around them. We hear nothing of Longbourn's parson; Mr Bennet does not behave like a squire, but none other is mentioned. The neighbouring great house, Netherfield Park, is available for let; why, we never learn. The Bennets' house has grounds mentioned (which spring into existence when Lady Catherine de Bourgh has a need to walk in them), and there appears to be a home farm, but there is no indication of who works it.[1] Mr Bennet, who seems to have no occupation whatever, is not seen performing any of the functions of a landowner, though his estate is large enough to sustain coveys of game birds.[2] His lack of a son and heir is necessary for reasons of plot, but that fact too serves to loosen him from attachment to his local habitation.

The sense of an inhabited locality is strongest in *Emma*: the village of Highbury is a more substantial presence than any of the towns and villages in the other completed novels. We find out more about its disposition; we hear about the names of the shops, the side road leading towards the vicarage, and so on; we are told who owns the land, the relation of Mr Woodhouse's property to the Donwell estate, the antecedents of both the Knightley and Woodhouse families[3]—such matters as *Pride and Prejudice*, with its brightly spotlit foreground, does not trouble about. R. W. Chapman, who tried hard enough, concluded that there was not quite enough evidence to draw a map of Highbury. That is just as well: it is not the novelist's business to be exhaustive, and one should always be suspicious of stories with maps attached to them—*The Lord of the Rings*, *Watership Down*, and (dare one say it?) the Wessexry of Thomas Hardy: the map-making all too often offers the reader a game to play as a substitute for a properly literary imagination. Jane Austen, justly disapproving of too many particulars of right hand and of left, gives us enough to convey a sense of solidity and ramification. The substance of Highbury is for her a means to an end; the human geography, so to speak, is what really concerns her. This is the one novel in which she gives us something like the whole of a small society. Literally, of course, that is not true—the poor and the servant class remain very much in the background—but what matters is that in this book she shows us her principal actors embedded in their society to some depth and with some complexity of root-formation.

This book is the happiest territory for those who want to see Jane Austen as a Tory philosopher, promoting an ideal vision of paternalism, hierarchy, ruralism, and social order. Actually, it seems a pretty odd interpretation even of *Emma*. Mr Knightley is undoubtedly a good landlord, but the other established rich man in the place, Mr Woodhouse, is a selfish, idle parasite (and that is the book's judgement, not an anachronistically modern verdict upon a society unlike our own); the spiritual welfare of the place is in the hands of a mean-spirited creep; the innocent Miss Bates, as Knightley himself points out, is likely to decline ever further into poverty and social degradation—is any of this the author's idea of society as it should be? It is indeed possible that she believed the present state of society to be the best that could be hoped for in a fallen world and that any likely change would be for the worse—I do not think that either the books or the letters give us enough evidence either way—but the notion that Highbury represents some sort of ideal is surely extraordinary. For what it may be worth, her nephew recorded that she took very little interest in the politics of the day, but he guessed that 'she probably shared the feeling of moderate Toryism which prevailed in her family'.[4] Her niece Caroline agreed that the general politics of the family were Tory, 'rather taken for granted I suppose, than discussed ... and in vain do I try to recall any word or expression of Aunt Jane's that had reference to public events— *Some* bias of course she *must* have had—but I can only *guess* to which quarter it inclined.'[5]

What the proponents of Jane Austen as Tory ideologue

should recognize, in any case, is that *Emma*, in giving so much substance to the society around the heroine, is unique among the novels. And I think it fair to say that here too her interest in a more fully depicted society is primarily as a new way of studying her principal actors. Mr Knightley is depicted as active in the management of estate, tenants, and more informal dependants—as none other of the heroes is—because that is the essence of what Knightley is and because that is the essence of the man that Emma will want to marry—the paternal type, who will be both like and unlike her real father. As for Emma herself, Jane Austen has previously given us the deracinated heroine (*Sense and Sensibility*), the heroine as mobile, a free spirit (*Pride and Prejudice*), the heroine in the house—and now she gives us the heroine in a small town.

The pervading presence of Highbury is used in a curiously and subtly double way. On the one hand, Emma is unique in the novels in being the queen of her society; on the other, she is like Fanny in being pent by her surroundings. Fanny, with her yearning to see Sotherton, her transparencies of Tintern, Cumberland, and Italy on the nursery window, knows that she is pent; Emma is pent without knowing it, and her story will be one of a liberation unlooked for and not even consciously desired. Emma is the only one of the heroines who is not in some sense a 'poor relation'. Anne Elliot is the other partial exception, and indeed Jane Austen's last two novels may be set beside one another as studies of privilege, in terms of birth and wealth, coexisting with emotional impoverishment. But Anne is the neglected one of the three Elliot sisters; Emma is unique in her authority and independence. Yet Emma's story should also be set beside *Mansfield Park*;

these two books, so different in tone and plot, so close in the time of their composition, make a pair as studies of imprisonment and eventual liberation.

Emma's imprisonment is a recurrent theme throughout the book, if we listen for it, never stressed, but suggested in all sorts of ways. It is a significant loss that Miss Taylor has gone half a mile away from her.[6] She says herself that she is hardly ever more than two hours from Hartfield.[7] She has never seen the sea; she has never even been to Box Hill, though this famous beauty spot is only half a dozen miles away.[8] Her father refuses to go to London, a mere sixteen miles distant,[9] and so she presumably is unable to go there (it is described as outside her daily reach, but since she is tied to her father's apron strings, it is hard to see how she can get there at all); this is in marked contrast to the mobile, restless Frank Churchill, who can ride to town and be back in a day. She is, along with Harriet and Mr Elton, 'fixed, so absolutely fixed, in the same place', without 'the power of removal'. She speaks to Mr Knightley about 'their confined society in Surry'. Mrs Elton is surprised that Emma gets out and about so little and tells her that she has lived 'so secluded a life'.[10] When John Knightley suggests that her social existence is expanding, she denies it with spirit: 'These amazing engagements of mine—what have they been? Dining once with the Coles—and having a ball talked of, which never took place.'[11]

She has no friends of her own age. Mrs Weston notices it: against Mr Knightley, she argues that it is good for Emma to have Harriet Smith as a companion—she is not the 'superior young woman which Emma's friend ought to be', but there is no one else.[12] Even Mrs Weston is much older than Emma;

and with her gone from Hartfield, the ladies she can regularly collect at home are Mrs Goddard, Miss Bates, and Miss Bates's aged mother[13]—her father's circle, in fact. Mr Knightley says that he would like to see her in love, but 'there is nobody hereabouts to attach her'. She herself laments the fact that there is no suitable young man in Highbury for Jane Fairfax to marry.[14] Though the place is a 'large and populous village almost amounting to a town', it has in fact been shrinking: a ballroom had been added to the Crown Inn when 'the neighbourhood had been in a particularly populous, dancing state', but 'such brilliant days had long passed away', and the space had been turned over to a men's whist club.[15] When Emma fears that Knightley may marry Harriet and thus 'the loss of Donwell' be inflicted on her, she asks herself 'what would remain of cheerful or of rational society within her reach'.[16]

About halfway through the story, Emma starts to become aware of some lack in her life. When she hears Frank Churchill praise Highbury, she feels that she has been used to despise Highbury too much.[17] That is a complex discovery. On the one hand, she appreciates her own village more, realizing that it offers a more decent society than that which Frank has experienced among his adoptive parents in Yorkshire. On the other hand she is starting to realize that actually she had felt frustration with that little world in which she had supposed herself to be content. When Frank leaves Highbury, she tries to analyse herself. She feels dull and listless, and at first thinks that she must be a little in love with Frank, but soon realizes that she is not.[18] We can see why she feels 'listlessness, weariness, stupidity', even if she herself cannot track down the cause: she is in a cage where her natural energies and affections are not able to fly free. Her life is too quiet, literally as well as metaphorically. In *Pride and Prejudice* we find the company planning 'a nice comfortable noisy game of lottery tickets'; in *Sense and Sensibility* we learn that Sir John Middleton likes to surround himself with noise: 'He delighted in collecting about him more young people than his house would hold, and the noisier they were the better he was pleased.'[19] These contrasts may remind us of what is lacking to Emma (and to the inhabitants of Mansfield Park, for that matter): enough good wholesome noise. There is indeed noise at Hartfield when her sister's children come to visit, but it is an affront to Mr Woodhouse, an interruption to the normal tenor of his and Emma's life.

Mr Woodhouse is one of Jane Austen's finest achievements. Of course, he has always been enjoyed—quite rightly—as one of her best comic creations, a lovable old silly, but her cleverness lies in making him at the same time a monster, the villain of the piece. I noted before that the first speaker in *Mansfield Park* is Mrs Norris. In *Emma* the first words of dialogue are given to Mr Woodhouse. And indeed there is an odd parallelism between these two so different figures: Mr Woodhouse too is the 'bad fairy' who has to be defeated if the heroine is to be happy. In his lack of vitality or zest for life the character in *Mansfield Park* whom Mr Woodhouse most resembles is Lady Bertram. But he comes nearest to Mrs Norris as an enemy of life and an enemy of other people's enjoyment.

It is illuminating to consider Mr Woodhouse in terms of the novel's structure. As we have seen, Jane Austen's plots in some formal respects show rather little variety. And just as each of the novels follows the basic pattern 'girl meets boy, girl marries boy', so each of them is supplied with a villain, whose machinations threaten the heroine's happiness: General Tilney, Lucy Steele, Wickham, Mrs Norris, William Walter Elliot, and in *Sanditon* Sir Edward Denham. Willoughby, though a more ambiguous case, might be added to the list, thus providing two villains for the novel with two heroines, though perhaps he should be rather be placed in the category most ripely realized in Henry Crawford: the moral agent who faces the choice of Hercules, between virtue and vice, and takes the wrong turning. The one apparent exception to this otherwise inexorable pattern is *Emma*. Here the two obviously nasty characters, Mrs Elton and her husband (the latter corrupted in the course of the narrative, but once corrupted, fixedly mean), do not count as villains in terms of the plot or story pattern, because they have no power over the heroine's life. Nonetheless, *Emma* is indeed no exception, because it does after all have a villain; and among Jane Austen's villains, Mr Woodhouse enjoys perhaps the longest and most continuous success of all.

He is also the stealthiest of the villains, so much so that many readers have not seen through him. In the film *Emma* he was portrayed as a rosy old buffer; I do not know how widespread that view of him remains. His monstrousness has been underestimated perhaps because the author is herself so stealthy, allowing into the text very few words overtly critical of him ('gentle selfishness', 'mild inexorability'), and even these tempered. A great deal of *Emma*, especially its later parts, is written in the form of interior monologue— another example of Jane Austen's originality and openness to experiments in technique. But with Mr Woodhouse she uses the theatrical method: his nature is revealed almost entirely through his own words and actions.

He is an adept at false solicitude. The first thing that we see him doing is stopping his daughter going to see her best friend: he inhibits Emma from visiting Mrs Weston at Randalls, and claims that it is out of consideration for his servant James. A couple of chapters later we learn the fraudulence of this: three of the local ladies 'were fetched and carried home so often that Mr. Woodhouse thought it no hardship for either James or the horses'.[20] He tries to get Mr Weston and Miss Taylor to postpone their wedding—solicitude again—because of the rain.[21] (This introduces another facet of his character, an impertinent officiousness which interferes in matters that are none of his business.) He tries to stop them having a wedding cake, and then to stop anyone eating it, supposedly from a tender concern for their digestion. The truth is that he is a solipsist, who 'could never believe other people to be different from himself. What was unwholesome to him, he regarded as unfit for any body . . .' The prospect of anyone eating cake disturbs his 'benevolent nerves', a nice phrase.[22]

He instinctively thinks of agreeable people as objects pleasant to himself. Jane Fairfax is 'a very pretty sort of young lady, a very pretty and a very well-behaved young lady indeed'. Tellingly, these are much the terms in which he has earlier described the housemaid: 'she is a civil, pretty-spoken girl . . . Whenever I see her, she always curtseys and asks me how I do, in a very pretty manner.'[23] But indeed, people only exist to serve his comfort, the gentlefolk no less than the servants. When Elton sends a 'long, civil, cere-monious note' to him, pointedly excluding Emma, she thinks that he is bound to notice the insult to his daughter; but he does not.[24] Though he is against matrimony, he never sees a marriage coming;[25] how could he, when he is interested in no person but himself? That incuriosity about anyone else makes him flatten out some very different characters into uniformity: he describes even Mrs Elton in the same terms as Jane Fairfax and the housemaid: 'considering we never saw her before, she seems a very pretty sort of young lady . . . She speaks a little too quick . . . However, she seems a very obliging, pretty-behaved young lady . . .'[26] There is in this a mixture of imperceptiveness and solipsism ('considering we never saw her before'—a person has no characteristics until she is before Mr Woodhouse's eyes).

'Every friend of Miss Taylor,' says Knightley, 'must be glad to have her so happily married.'[27] That lets the cat out of the bag. Mr Woodhouse is no friend to her, but indeed her most implacable enemy, who would ruthlessly have destroyed her hope of happiness, given the chance. Moreover, his attitude towards her reveals another of his characteristics: his inexorability. Like the Japanese soldier in the jungle refusing to believe in his country's surrender, he declines to accept that she is married: Miss Taylor she remains—indeed 'poor Miss Taylor', for his colossal egoism will not accept that anyone can be happy who has separated herself from his society. He is against life: thus he is depressed by his elder daughter Isabella's attachment to her husband—sex is another of the things he is against—and instead of delighting in the ordinary, boisterous pleasures of his grandchildren, he frets about them.[28] And if one thinks about it, his opposition to all marriage is a brutal insult to the memory of his wife. Indeed, it implies something about the nature of his marriage. No word is said about that, but we do learn from Mr Knightley's mouth that his wife was talented; this is where Emma has got her quickness and cleverness from.[29] We might reflect on what the character of her life is likely to have been, once she realized what sort of man she had married. In *Persuasion* we are told explicitly that the heroine's late mother strove to do the best she could with the desolating discovery that her husband was vacuous;[30] in *Emma* we are left to infer it.

Mr Woodhouse is against life's homelier pleasures too. He 'would have made a difficulty if he could', we are told at one point, about some simple arrangement.[31] Recurrently he stops people eating.[32] Miss Bates describes one such occasion:[33]

> There was a little disappointment.—The baked apples and biscuits, excellent in their way, you know; but there was a delicate fricassee of sweetbread and some asparagus brought in at first, and good Mr. Woodhouse, not thinking the asparagus quite boiled enough, sent it all out again. Now there is nothing grandmamma loves better than sweetbread and asparagus—so she was rather disappointed, but we agreed we would not speak of it to anybody . . .

That was a good evening's work for Mr Woodhouse—depriving a poor old woman of one of her few enjoyments. It is also significant that he has fooled Miss Bates ('*good* Mr. Woodhouse') into a belief in his beneficence: he is not only a fraud but a successful fraud. Jane Austen knows, however, that his obsession over food is not only valetudinarianism but *gourmandise*, the fussiness of a perverted epicureanism. He insists that apples must be baked: it is the only way that he thinks the fruit thoroughly wholesome.[34] C. S. Lewis's

Screwtape notes that there is a gluttony of delicacy as well as a gluttony of excess; Mr Woodhouse is a glutton of delicacy.

We are assured that he is 'everywhere beloved for the friendliness of his heart and his amiable temper'. His 'good nature' is listed, along with his money and the appeal of his daughter, as one of the causes why he can draw others to himself.[35] But there are indications that others' view of him is not quite so uniformly favourable. Thus it is made evident that John Knightley, despite his 'great regard for his father-in-law, and generally a strong sense of what was due to him', finds him extremely irritating; and on one blessed occasion he exploits Mr Woodhouse's nervousness to bully him, 'pursuing his triumph rather unfeelingly'.[36] Some phrases are ambiguous: 'Papa is only speaking his own regret,' Emma explains, after Mr Woodhouse has implied that Mrs Weston is none too well. Perhaps she says more than she intends.[37] 'You quite forget Mr Weston,' she adds a little later, after her father has complained that though Mrs Weston comes to see him often, she is always obliged to go away again. Indeed: he 'forgets' the interests of anyone other than himself. Mrs Weston's own true feelings also break out toward the end of the book: no one but Mr Knightley, she reflects, could 'know and bear with Mr. Woodhouse'.[38] We might reflect, in turn, that before her marriage she had been compelled to know and bear with Mr Woodhouse for many years: 'poor Miss Taylor', after all. At the end of the book, part of Emma's liberation is that she can now see through her father. Before, we have overheard her telling herself that her father's tenderness of nature is what has made him generally loved. Now she can mimic his silliness (with affection to be sure) as she has mimicked others in her world: 'I wish I may not sink into "poor Emma" with him at once.—His tender compassion towards oppressed worth can go no farther.'[39] There is some ambiguity about that last sentence, but it sounds as though Emma has at last begun to recognize how limited and superficial is his supposed kindliness.

He is an octopus whose tentacles draw others towards himself. His rank and wealth enable him to 'command the visits of his own little circle'.[40] He has succeeded in making the world revolve around his person: everyone must spend time and trouble thinking about him. When the Westons, for example, want to give a dinner party, it is he who determines that the hours must be early and the numbers few, his 'habits and inclination being consulted in every thing'.[41] It is not enough for him to have his own comforts satisfied: his employment is to destroy the pleasures of others. In his own words, 'the sooner every party breaks up, the better.'[42] At the Donwell strawberry party, he is supplied with a comfortable room set up for his convenience, 'Books of engravings, drawers of medals, cameos, corals, shells' and other curios are produced to entertain him, but it is not enough: to complete his pleasure he must damage that of others. Mrs Weston must sit with him, deprived of the enjoyment of the sunny summer gardens, until Emma (a sign, incidentally, of her unobtrusive kindness) comes to relieve her.[43]

Is this account of Mr Woodhouse too hard on him? It might be objected that he is too passive a personality to be the active force of malignancy that I have represented. It might be objected too that if he is as malignant as I have said, why is he so well beloved? But it is in these very paradoxes that Jane Austen's brilliance lies. At first sight Mr Woodhouse may seem to be a first-rate comic cut, very amusing but no more. But Jane Austen's wit, and her psychological penetration, show that his passivity is aggressive and rapacious. There are, as we have seen, some hints that Mr Woodhouse may not be altogether as well beloved as Emma supposes, but certainly he commands a fair bit of affection. And indeed there is something charming and lovable about the old boy. So amiable and yet a monster—the genius of the portrayal lies in just this, that both things are true. There is both likeness and unlikeness to the way in which Jane Austen has handled Fanny Price. This most passive of heroines turns into a 'daemon'. That, of course, is Mrs Norris's view, and Fanny is genuinely good; the portrait of Mr Woodhouse examines in a different way the idea first discovered and explored in *Mansfield Park*, of how passivity may become power. Mr Woodhouse is also remarkably in advance of his time as a study of subconscious motivation. I have described him as a villain and a destroyer, but we are not to imagine, of course, that he has clearly articulated his motives to himself. Nor is his amiability feigned. The interplay of conscious and unconscious motives is very finely observed; that is why he can be both so ineffectual and so dangerous, such a menace and such a dear.

But he remains a bloodsucker, fastened upon his daughter's flesh. In *Clueless* (the film comedy which transfers the *Emma* story to modern Los Angeles) the father is made into a successful, driven lawyer, very unlike the idle potterer in the book; but this film does seem to understand, as the other film versions of *Emma* do not, both that the father is needed by his daughter, as the object on which a warm heart can expend its natural affection, and that he is an incubus. Mr Woodhouse's crime is to use his daughter's love for himself in a plot to blight her life, if he can. We know that he is hostile to all matrimony, and we can see how near he comes to succeeding with Emma when she explains to Harriet why she means never to marry:[44]

> Fortune I do not want; employment I do not want; consequence I do not want; I believe few married women are half as much mistress of their husband's house, as I am of Hartfield; and never, never could I expect to be so truly beloved and important; so always first and always right in any man's eyes as I am in my father's.

Mr Woodhouse, that is to say, has been wrapping Emma in flattery as a spider wraps a fly. Harriet's response—that Emma will turn into an old maid—may seem merely conventional, but ironically she is the one showing sense this time.

Mr Woodhouse fails to prevent Emma's engagement, but he fights on to prevent her happiness to the last, and he is defeated, thanks to the incident in the poultry-yard, only on the very last page. Even then, the victory is not complete, for though he has finally allowed Emma to marry her lover, he has required them to live in his house. Knightley must quit his beloved Donwell, and Emma must still live with the man who has shackled her. (It is amusing to find that Jane Austen is reported, in private conversation, to have taken pity on them and killed Mr Woodhouse off after a couple of years; but that lies outside the novel.[45])

What then of Emma herself? A recent book may well be representing a common view when it describes this novel as one 'in which the sins of selfishness and snobbery might receive their just rebuke'.[46] It is indeed an old opinion:

'Emma is, of course, an inveterate snob,' says Marvin Mudrick flatly ('of course'!).[47] But to call Emma selfish is carelessness: she is after Anne Elliot the most self-giving of the heroines, and she is eager to be useful. She is not a snob either in most senses of the term. It is true that she thinks social distinctions ought to be observed: Frank Churchill is a little too indifferent to 'confusions of rank', and the Coles ought to know their place;[48] but Emma thinks these things essentially because she is jealous of her position as the ruler of her tiny kingdom. That is indeed a fault, but snobbery is not exactly the word for it. Like Julius Caesar, she would rather be first in a village than second at Rome: she has no ambition whatever to raise herself beyond the circumscribed conditions of her life by a good marriage—indeed she thinks she does not want to marry at all, but says that she is content, as we have seen, to remain mistress of Hartfield, beloved and important in her father's eyes.[49] By contrast, Mrs Elton is indeed a snob, and Emma finds her snobbery repulsive. It is Mrs Elton who goes on about 'first circles, spheres, lines, ranks, every thing'—all the apparatus of social self-consciousness.[50] Except when she is in a cross mood, Emma seems almost as much indifferent to rank as Frank can be. Far from scorning the dim, illegitimate Harriet, she wants her to share as much as possible of her own experience.[51] Her best friend is a woman who has escaped from the despised status of a governess by marrying a parvenu. Mr Weston is not a gentleman, but it does not signify; and Emma day-dreams about marrying Frank Churchill, Mr Weston's son, even before meeting him.

What then is it that Emma learns? What 'sin' is rebuked? I think that what she discovers is essentially the autonomy of other people. She has believed that she knows what people are and how their lives should proceed. If Robert Martin were in truth what Emma has decided that he is, if Harriet were in truth what Emma has decided that she is or might become, then indeed they ought not to marry; but actually she is wrong about both of them. In one respect, perhaps, she is her father's daughter, in supposing that people's desires and interests are as she has determined they shall be. The difference, of course, is that Mr Woodhouse's determinations are the product of selfishness, Emma's of a misguided benevolence. What she learns is that we must leave people be and let them follow the laws of their own natural growth. She wants to improve Harriet, but she manipulates her without Harriet's knowing what is being done to her. Mr Knightley wants to improve Emma, but he goes about it openly: he speaks to her face, in the hope of making her what she can—properly, naturally—become.

Emma is perhaps the least strongly sexed of the heroines. And maybe she is the only one among them not to be a great reader. (Lizzy Bennet denies being a great reader when accused of it by Miss Bingley, but her standard is likely to be high, and some words from Darcy a little later imply that he supposes her to read a lot.) Emma does read, of course (Jane Austen could perhaps not have borne to create a heroine who did not read at all), but her reading, like her music and her drawing, is fitful and irregular; it does not meet Mr Knightley's standards, though these are likely to be demanding.[52] She will never read steadily, he says, because she will not submit to 'a subjection of the fancy to the understanding'. This suggests an easy, carefree temperament. It is perhaps unlucky that Jane Austen's casual remark about creating a heroine whom no one would much like except herself has been so often quoted, because it has encouraged people to expect to find Emma unappealing. This misconception has affected the film adaptations: Emma as played by Gwyneth Paltrow is insipid and dully supercilious, while in the television version she is merely sour. Here again it is *Clueless* which understands the book best—the only version to appreciate that Emma is affectionate, lovable, lively, fun to be with. Indeed, the story hardly makes sense unless we understand Emma in this way. Everyone in the book likes her—everyone, that is, except the odious Mrs Elton, and Mr Elton, of course, once he has been rejected. She is subtly poised between self-criticism and an aversion to self-criticism: we see this in the way in which she seems to invite Mr Knightley to find fault with her (there is of course a sexual element to this which she does not yet understand), and in her technique of pre-empting criticism by coquettish confession of her weaknesses. She has a 'happy disposition'; that is the very first thing we are told about her character, in the very first sentence of the book. She is interested in people, and humorously observant of them, as we see from her lively mimicry of their little tricks of speech. She wants people to be happy, even at a cost to herself: though she misses Miss Taylor greatly, she rejoices in her marriage and believes that it was she who 'made the match'. She wants to be useful to Harriet, misguidedly of course, but honestly.[53] She also resolves on an enormous sacrifice, as no other of the heroines does: if Mr Knightley asks her about Harriet's feeling, she will tell him that his love for Harriet (as she supposes it to be) is returned.[54] Emma seems born to be a heroine of romantic comedy: that is one reason why the puzzle about how the story can turn out happily creates suspense. In the event, *Emma*, like *Mansfield Park*, conforms to the character of its heroine: *Mansfield Park* is solemn and serious, while *Emma* is lively and full of fun.

I have suggested that we may best understand some of these novels by supposing that the author wants to develop different kinds of emotional tone and colour—in particular, that the special character of *Mansfield Park* is most likely due not to some radical change in Jane Austen's outlook or to some crisis in her life, but to a wish to range more widely, to explore another part of the forest. A similar principle may help to illuminate *Emma*. In spirit this book seems to move well away from the depressed tone of *Mansfield Park* back to the sparkle of *Pride and Prejudice*, but the two later novels, written so close in time to one another, are the closest also in terms of basic underlying plot. There is a kind of musical analysis which seeks to strip away almost everything— rhythm, harmony, most of the melody—to establish the work's most fundamental and simple idea. If we try something like this with *Mansfield Park* and *Emma*, we find that both do not exactly follow the girl-meets-boy pattern, because girl has always known boy. In each the heroine marries a man whom she has known closely and seen constantly for almost all of her life.

It is Jane Austen's mastery, and her pleasure, to show how profoundly she can vary one basic plot idea (a difficult idea, what is more: the quick burgeoning romance of an Elizabeth and her Darcy is so much easier to manage). *Emma* and *Mansfield Park* are the two longest of the novels, and it should therefore seem surprising that they are also the two which compress the courtship between hero and heroine into

the shortest space. Both books take the risk of unusual pro-
portions, but in opposite ways. Fanny's attachment to
Edmund spreads across the whole length of the book, continues unrequited for years, and even so, the courtship, as we
have seen, is hidden from us, and pushed into a sort of postscript. In the later novel, by contrast, Mr Knightley's proposal comes very soon after Emma has realized that she is in
love with him. It also comes much further from the end of the
book than in the other novels. Jane Austen is almost unique
among novelists in her capacity to make her form expressive,
to use it as a vehicle to convey a book's ethos. *Mansfield Park*
is much concerned with endurance; and so Fanny's most
important emotional state remains more or less unchanging
throughout the action. *Emma* is much concerned with
development, and it is all mobility (mobile in mood and
impression, that is, since Emma is physically the most static
of all the heroines).

Fittingly this book is more spacious after Mr Knightley's
proposal because there is to be more development in Emma
between her engagement and her marriage, and we are to
learn more about her. The effect of these fifty or so pages is
that we see her liberation, her blossoming; and it is beautiful
and moving. We behold her lit up with an inward hilarity.
For example, earlier in the story she has been concerned
that Mr Knightley should not marry because that would
mean that her nephew, who is also his, would probably
lose the hope of inheriting Donwell. But now the case is
altered:[55]

> It is remarkable, that Emma, in the many, the very many,
> points of view in which she was now beginning to consider
> Donwell Abbey, was never struck with any sense of injury to

her nephew Henry, whose rights as heir expectant had formerly been so tenaciously regarded. Think she must of the possible difference to the poor little boy; and yet she only gave herself a saucy conscious smile about it, and found amusement in detecting the real cause of that violent dislike of Mr Knightley's marrying Jane Fairfax, or any body else, which at the time she had wholly imputed to the amiable solicitude of the sister and the aunt.

Most novelists, I think, would have had the lady indulge in a little penitence or at least sober reflection here. But Emma just cannot repent. She thinks the thing simply *funny*. And she finds herself funny; there are both a lightness and a maturity of self-knowledge in that—both a continuation and a transformation of her earlier self-questioning—which are irresistibly attractive. Her spirits are also dancing, to be sure, with the hope of motherhood—this is one of the very few places where Jane Austen looks forward to the possibility of one of her heroines having children. And the indication here, as on those other rare occasions, is very light and oblique.

Jane Austen allows Emma's gaiety to infect the narrative voice itself. In the other novels the heroine answers the hero's proposal with seriousness and confusion, but this time the author breaks the tension with a laugh: 'What did she say?—Just what she ought, of course. A lady always does.'[56] The narrative has represented the flow of Emma's consciousness for so long that we feel this to be her own voice, triumphing and teasing herself in one and the same breath. Later, when she learns that Harriet is to marry Robert Martin after all, her blitheness soars even higher: 'She wanted to be alone. Her mind was in a state of flutter and

171

wonder which made it impossible for her to be collected. She was in dancing, singing, exclaiming spirits; and till she had moved about and talked to herself, and laughed and reflected, she could be fit for nothing rational.'[57] We might pause to notice that her essential aloneness remains. She needs to talk, to exclaim: Lizzy Bennet would have talked and exclaimed to her sister Jane, but Emma has no other person to share her gaiety with, and no desire for one. This conversation with herself, this solitary dance of rapture without a partner, enchants with that sort of blitheness that can seem not far from poignancy.

Jane Austen's earliest readers would probably have expected a good deal more moralizing, and she is bold to eschew it. Emma has of course felt 'perplexity and distress' about how to break the news of her own engagement to Harriet, and passed through 'every bitter reproach and sorrowful regret'.[58] But much of this is a question of social awkwardness and a desire to be as kind as possible; Emma seems, on the whole, to feel rather little guilt. That seems fine and true: sheer joy overwhelms every other feeling and the *égoisme à deux* of love crowds out all other emotions. Most writers, I think, would have presented the news of Harriet's engagement as above all a relief, the loss of a burden. Jane Austen does not quite exclude that idea, but it is subordinated to gaiety. Emma's light spirits become even lighter. Once more, she thinks the thing simply funny: she laughs. Harriet and her past treatment of Harriet are such a joke:[59]

> Serious she was, very serious in her thankfulness, and in her resolutions; and yet there was no preventing a laugh, some-times in the very midst of them. She must laugh at such a

close! Such an end to the doleful disappointment of five weeks back! Such a heart—such a Harriet!

The difference in flavour between *Emma* and *Mansfield Park* may be brought out, for one last time, by a similarity. 'Poor Sir Thomas,' the author exclaims, as the issue is resolved in the earlier book; and 'Poor Mr Woodhouse' she echoes in the latter. Sir Thomas, we saw, was not so far from becoming a tragic figure, but how differently Jane Austen treats Emma's father: 'Poor Mr Woodhouse little suspected what was plotting against him in the breast of that man whom he was so cordially welcoming, and so anxiously hoping might not have taken cold from the ride.'[60] Like Emma smiling at the thought of blighting the hopes of her nephew, we cannot help delighting in Mr Woodhouse's discomfiture, with that very proper denial of sympathy which is the essence of high comedy. The parody of the language of high drama—the implication that Mr Knightley designs treachery, the 'impending evil' that will be spoken of in the next sentence—encourages us to this happy hardening of the heart.

6

The Sense in Sensibility

With *Mansfield Park* and *Emma* Jane Austen achieved a refinement and facility such as neither she nor any other novelist had reached before. We might expect to find these qualities continued in her last completed work, but this is only partially so. *Persuasion*, a book which can command a special kind of affection, does represent in some technical ways a falling off from its three wonderful predecessors, and one may speculate whether the onset of illness was beginning to weaken Jane Austen's stamina. For one thing, it is that great rarity, a novel which is too short. (The fault may be as rare in music also: Purcell's *Dido and Aeneas* is perhaps the only great piece of music—and it is indeed among the greatest—which ideally requires to be longer than it is.) *Persuasion* is, like *Mansfield Park*, a novel about lonely endurance, and we really need to live through Anne Elliot's endurance more extensively than the book allows us to; and one might wish that the reawakening of Wentworth's love for her had been a more gradual process.

The plot of *Persuasion* may well be superior, in neatness and plausibility, to those of almost all nineteenth-century novels; nonetheless, it is not quite up to Jane Austen's highest standards. The William Walter Elliot subplot is oddly inconsequential. The attempt to integrate it with the main plot—we are to suppose that Wentworth has been put off from declaring his renewed love by jealousy of Mr Elliot—seems a little thin, and Mr Elliot's own motive—to prevent Sir Walter marrying again by marrying his daughter and using 'the watchfulness which a son-in-law's right would have given'[1]—is forced: rich, handsome widowers marry again, or not, to suit themselves. Wentworth is oddly feeble and unmanned when the accident occurs at Lyme; this seems out of character for a tough, successful naval man (he is, after all, the first man of action among the heroes since Colonel Brandon).

Persuasion is much the shortest of Jane Austen's novels, except for *Northanger Abbey*, which is obviously a special case, and all of them are compact by the standards of the day—the standard of Fanny Burney and Maria Edgeworth, that is to say. It does seem likely that her energy was starting to decline, and that she did the best she could; and in the case of an author so controlled and self-aware it is tempting to go further and suggest that she was conscious of some deficiency. There may be a parallel earlier in her career. As it stands *Lady Susan* is a novella in epistolary form, about seventy pages long, but it reads as though it had originally been planned to be longer, perhaps much longer. It seems plausible to suppose that Jane Austen realized in the course of writing that the devices of telling the story in letters and of having a villainess as the principal character were ones which she could not or did not care to sustain over the length of a full novel; and at a somewhat arbitrary point the tale is rounded off and brought to a curt conclusion. She made no attempt to publish *Lady Susan*, but we know that she made a fair copy of it in 1805 or thereabouts; whether the actual writing took place then or much earlier is uncertain, but in either case it seems clear that she thought she had done work good enough to be worth preserving. It looks as if she found herself unable or unwilling to carry through her original intention, but still wanted to bring the work to completion and move on. And I suspect that she felt similarly at the time of writing *Persuasion*: if the book could not have the scope and amplitude of *Mansfield Park* or *Emma*, let it at least be finished.

If this guess is right, it may lead on to two kinds of reflection. The first concerns tone. In the opening chapter we learn that Anne's dead mother had not been 'the very happiest being in the world herself' but 'had found enough in her duties, her friends, and her children, to attach her to life, and make it no matter of indifference to her when she was called on to quit them'. If we suppose that the writer of these cool words knew herself to be ill and was perhaps beginning to contemplate the prospect of an early death, they acquire a stoical, ironic courage. (Stern critical doctrine may tell us that we should not let our judgement of a literary work be affected by some fact that we happen to know about the author's circumstances, still less by uncertain speculation, but let us yield to human weakness.) This consideration may even make us more understanding of what is perhaps the most painful slip in tone and moral balance in the whole canon—the harsh assertion that the Musgroves have had 'the good fortune to lose' their troublesome, useless son Dick, sent away to sea and luckily dead at the age of 18.[2] (Two chapters after this pitiless dismissal comes the strange scene in which Jane Austen mocks fat, silly Mrs Musgrove for lamenting her son while at the same time apologizing for her mockery—an odd and puzzling passage.) Those coming near to death have more licence to slight its importance.

The second reflection growing from the hypothesis that Jane Austen was already aware of ebbing strength concerns *Sanditon*. The more ill we suppose her to have been when she started *Sanditon*, the more it may appear as a work of desperate courage, rather than the fragment of a larger design which she lacked the time and health to complete. In other words, she may not have had the plot and scope of her new work fully worked out, and what we have may be rather a scrambling together of bits and pieces looking for direction. This is perhaps a disappointing thought, as it would be attractive to believe that *Sanditon* provided good evidence of how Jane Austen habitually worked. But her creative processes remain opaque. The one case where we do know exactly how she rewrote a section confounds expectation: anyone would suppose that the scene in which Wentworth overhears Anne talking to Captain Harville was part of the novel's plan from the beginning, perhaps the original germ from which it grew. In fact, it was an afterthought.

Jane Austen resists our curiosity in some other respects too. It is a paradox that her books have inspired so much interest in the life of their author, for she is among the least autobiographical of novelists. None of her family, we are told, recognized any of their acquaintances in her books, though there were some among them who cried out for comic treatment.³ Weak or otherwise inadequate fathers appear in several of her books; the personality of George Austen seems to be lost to us, but there is no reason to think that he was at all like Mr Bennet, Mr Woodhouse, Sir Thomas Bertram, Mr Price, or Sir Walter Elliot, who indeed, though all unsatisfactory fathers in one way or another, are a strikingly varied lot. We know a little more about Mrs Austen, a strong, humorous, and intelligent person; there is no such mother in the novels, though it is possible that bits of her get into some of Jane's portraits of older women.

The nineteenth-century English novel sees the greatest achievement by women in the literature of Europe since Sappho twenty-five centuries earlier. This efflorescence of talent is so familiar to us, and has come to seem so natural, that we may easily forget the obstacles in the way of women succeeding in this field, not from lack of opportunity to learn their craft or do their work, as may have been the case in some other fields of artistic endeavour, but from lacking the diversity of knowledge and experience needed to give range and depth to their books. The difficulty was most acute for a novelist like Jane Austen who was not willing to describe what lay outside her own experience: famously she never, except for one tiny instant in *Mansfield Park*, shows us men on their own, without a woman present. This is in part due to her subjective manner of writing: much of the time we see the action through a particular pair of eyes, and with brief and unimportant exceptions these are female in the completed novels. Our access to Sir Edward Denham's reveries is a new departure in *Sanditon*; his daydreams of seduction or rape provide one of the most unexpected moments in Jane

Austen's writing. When she did have access to expert knowledge of a masculine sphere, she used it: the naval talk in *Mansfield Park* and *Persuasion* rings with an impressive authenticity.

A particular problem for a woman author was her lack of all those years of Greek and Latin with which an educated gentleman's mind was furnished. When the Prince Regent's librarian urged Jane Austen to take a virtuous and literary clergyman for a hero, she replied that such a man's conversation would necessarily be often upon science and philosophy, subjects of which she knew little; and no author could do justice to such a character without having enjoyed a classical education himself.[4] Jane Austen simply leaves this aspect of male experience out, and on the whole she was wise. As great a writer as George Eliot was a little damaged as an artist by the disabilities of being a woman: excluded from what she once called 'the Eleusinian mysteries of a university education',[5] she could not resist the impulse to show off her self-taught erudition (which was indeed an astonishing achievement of will and intellect). Jane Austen, by contrast, simply rests her confidence in the innate quality of her mind. In *Persuasion*, when Anne Elliot talks to Captain Harville—in the interchange overheard by Wentworth, which leads him to propose to her—we realize that we are hearing something rare in literature: an intelligent, equal, and entirely serious conversation between a man and a woman. Almost any other writer would have had them talk about literature and politics (George Eliot would have had them discussing Sophocles), but Jane Austen is content to demonstrate the heroine's intelligence—and able to bring the demonstration off—in a conversation simply about human relations.

All of the heroines are distinctly intelligent (except Catherine Morland) or at the least are eager to read and learn (and this does include Catherine): Emma is called clever in the book's first sentence, and Elizabeth Bennet is so obviously clever that there is no need to say it. The heroes are harder to estimate, though none of them lacks sense. There does remain a problem with the presentation of the male characters, one that arises also with another novelist of especial subtlety, Henry James. James has the frequent habit of telling us that his characters are so finely, so wonderfully clever (a bad habit, for it is the novelist's task to show us this, not to let assertion substitute for demonstration), but we are commonly left wondering what this cleverness is exercised on, and what body of knowledge sustains it. The consequence is a kind of hollowness: the minds of his people are at once oversophisticated and underfurnished—a reminder that James, despite his time at Harvard, was mostly self-taught, and that for all his cosmopolitan upbringing and deep penetration into England's cultural life, he came to his adopted country after reaching adulthood, from the outside.

Jane Austen does not often tell us about her people's education. Two of her baddies, Wickham and Henry Crawford, were at Cambridge; two of the heroes, Henry Tilney and Edmund Bertram, as well as the innocuous James Morland and the deeply stupid John Thorpe, are Oxford men. (When Fanny Price passes through Oxford without stopping on the way from Mansfield to Southampton, she gets a hasty glimpse of Edmund's college.[6] This may be a private reference for the family: the route through the town from north to south would have taken Fanny past the front gates of only two of the twenty odd colleges, but one of them would have been St John's, the college at which the Austens were founder's kin, attended by Jane's father and her brothers James and Henry.) One of the heroes (Edmund Bertram) was schooled at Eton, and two of the baddies (Henry Crawford and Robert Ferrars) at Westminster. Edward Ferrars was privately educated, at 'Mr Pratt's'.

It is a merit in Jane Austen that she does not clog up the narrative with insignificant detail (yet again, one may recall her remark to young Anna, protesting against 'too many particulars of left hand and of right'), and it is no fault in her that she supplies so little information about her people's schools and universities. The doubt lies elsewhere. Many of her characters are so solidly conceived that she seems to have imagined and realized their whole being. But she does not present the effects of education on those of her people who might be expected to show it. Frank Churchill is the only one to use a Latin tag, when he refers to his 'amor patriae'. Darcy 'cannot comprehend the neglect of a family library in such days as these', but we are not told what the books are with which he has been stocking Pemberley.[7] And what kinds of work are they that Mr Bennet spends his days reading? It may be that Jane Austen has an idea of how these people are furnishing their minds, but if so, she does not share it with us. It is different with her women: true, we would not know that Emma has read Madame de Genlis, or that Fanny is reading Crabbe's poems and Macartney's memoir of China, if the author had not told us, but even when we do not pick up information of this kind, we usually feel with her best characters that they continue in being when they are no longer on the page. That applies to the grotesques as well: Mrs Elton and Mrs Norris, Mr Collins and Lady Catherine. But one cannot quite restrain the feeling that when Darcy and Mr Bennet have closed the doors of their libraries behind them, they no longer exist, even though Mr Bennet, at least, is one of Jane Austen's profoundest studies.

For the most part her depiction of ordinary men and manners is outstandingly accurate, complete, and solid, but when it comes to politics, she is sketchy. Henry Tilney talks fluently to Catherine about landscape and the picturesque, but then 'he shortly found himself arrived at politics; and from politics, it was an easy step to silence'.[8] That is appropriately amusing (Catherine is half a child still and Henry is 'fearful of wearying her with too much wisdom at once'); it is when politics impinges on more serious or substantial characters that we may start to suspect that Jane Austen has not thought the circumstances right through as she usually does, better indeed than almost any other novelist. Few of her men show any overt interest in politics, though Henry Crawford talks it with Dr Grant.[9] Fanny Price, the most widely curious of the heroines, is perhaps the only woman to show any interest in a social or political issue, with her questions to Sir Thomas about the slave trade. Sir Thomas himself is a Member of Parliament, though there seems to be no way of telling which interest he represents. Mr Palmer, in *Sense and Sensibility*, is standing for Parliament, and we learn, rather to our surprise, that Willoughby is attached to the other side, but once again there appears to be no knowing which party is whose. Perhaps we do not need to know the allegiances of Palmer and Willoughby, but one would like to feel quite confident that Jane herself knew.

Jane Austen was extremely intelligent without being in

the least an intellectual. However, there is sometimes a reluctance among professors to suppose that men and women of genius can be people very unlike themselves. Like Emma Woodhouse and Lady Catherine de Bourgh, academics also want to be useful: and if the currents of contemporary moral, social, and political debate flow through a novel, a delightfully didactic prospect opens. But the attempt to recruit Jane Austen into one of the armies in an ideological war is mistaken. There were of course radical novelists writing in her time. There were also conservative moralists, whom modern scholarship has drawn out of a deep obscurity, such as Mrs West, author of novels entitled *The Advantages of Education, A Gossip's Story* (narrated by Prudentia Homespun), and *A Tale of the Times* (in which the heroine is raped and dies of shame), and Mrs Hamilton, author such novels as *Letters of a Hindoo Rajah, Memoirs of Modern Philosophers* (in which the heroine is seduced by a revolutionary and dies of a broken heart), and *The Cottagers of Glenburnie*.[10] These do not sound much like Jane Austen even superficially. It is indeed useful to compare her to her contemporaries, but for another reason: to confirm her originality and independence, and appreciate how distinctively absent ideology is from her fiction. She ranks not among those novelists like Tolstoy and George Eliot who are in some sense teachers or preachers, but among those like James and Proust, for whom the depiction and analysis of human beings in thought and action are enough. Or in different terms, she is of the school of Sophocles and Shakespeare, not that of Dante and Milton. I mention these lofty names to confute the claim that if she was not engaged in the struggle of ideas, she was not doing her job properly.

Her nephew put the matter sensibly in his memoir, with this estimate of the novels: 'They certainly were not written to support any theory or inculcate any particular moral, except indeed that great moral which is to be equally gathered from an observation of the course of actual life—namely, the superiority of high over low principles, and of greatness over littleness of mind.'[11]

Jane Austen was indeed concerned with men and women as moral beings, facing moral choices. But insofar as her books present a general idea or theory of how we should conduct ourselves, it is one that is less prim and rational than many of her interpreters have supposed. To confront this issue squarely, we need to go back to her earlier career, to *Sense and Sensibility*. This is the work which may seem best to vindicate the belief that she ranges herself on one side in a war of moral ideas. Does it not claim to demonstrate that Sense is right, and Sensibility wrong? This is a tricky question, not least because *Sense and Sensibility* is the one novel in which Jane Austen does not seem to be fully in control of her effect. It is a puzzling, uneasy book, in part because it may be more complex and ambiguous than some critics have realized, but also perhaps because its intention has not been entirely carried out.

Its earlier version bore the title *Elinor and Marianne*. This surely does not suggest an antithesis like *Sandford and Merton* (the nice boy and the nasty boy) or the cartoon *Tom and Jerry* (bad cat and good mouse) but a pairing on terms of something like moral equality. We might compare another nineteenth-century novel with a paired antithesis in its title: Mrs Gaskell's *North and South*. In this the heroine, like Jane Austen the daughter of a Hampshire parson, goes north to

Milton (a thinly disguised Manchester), where she meets and eventually marries a self-made manufacturer. The book plays with a number of dichotomies, north and south, culture and energy, masculine and feminine, art and action, Catholicism and dissent, and essential to its success is that each side of each dichotomy is treated with respect. Thornton (the industrialist) and Margaret Hale (the heroine) learn each from the other, and in their union the virtues of North and South are combined. David Lodge's witty updating of this story, *Nice Work*, similarly depicts the relationship between a down-to-earth manufacturer and a trendy female academic, but though the book can show her teaching him, it fails to imagine anything that he can teach her, a failure which damages its moral breadth and balance. Mrs Gaskell manages better to preserve an equipoise; and we might expect Jane Austen's poise to be at least as fine.

Elinor and Marianne are contrasted in outlook and temperament, but Jane Austen adds to this a formal contrast. Elinor is the focalizer, the pair of eyes through whom most of the action is seen, but Marianne is the emotional centre of the book, the one who has the adventures, whereas Elinor's role is largely reactive. There is thus an asymmetry between the two heroines in terms of narrative presentation. In this way Jane Austen makes things more interesting for herself, but also more difficult. The danger with a paired antithesis is that it can look too tidy and artificial; the danger with Jane Austen's asymmetry is that it may give too much weight to the values of the focalizing character. It is not a danger that she entirely escapes. But it is worth pondering the possibility that the weight upon Elinor may be due as much to an experiment in form as to her being right, Marianne wrong.

And inescapably the emotional heart of the book is Marianne, which might lead us to question the notion that we are asked to reject outright everything that she is and that she values. One apparent way out of the difficulty is to argue that Jane Austen uses 'sensibility' to mean not the cultivation of aesthetic awareness and passionate enjoyment but the abuse of such aspirations. 'Sensibility' would thus be a term something like 'political correctness', that is to say, a term used ironically. More often than not, the words 'politically correct' are used not favourably, but within implicit inverted commas, with the connotation of censoriousness and sanctimony. Similarly, anti-romantics might use 'sensibility' to mean pretentiousness, gush, or the affectation of sensibility.

But this supposed solution of the difficulty only makes matters worse. The book ought not to be comparing Sense and Silliness, or Sense and Self-Indulgence: if that is what it does, it surely awards Sense too cheap and easy a victory. Like Milton's *L'Allegro* and *Il Penseroso*, Sense and Sensibility should each be states of mind for which a good case can be made; and which each may be subject to some faults or weakness. Jane Austen does indeed make a little fun of Sense as well as Sensibility. When Marianne shows Edward the loveliness of the Devon countryside, he replies, 'It is a beautiful country . . .; but these bottoms must be dirty in winter.'[12] This is plonkingly prosaic, and displays the limitations of too much Sense in the absence of the complementary quality. It is a fair criticism of the book, however, that these limitations are not shown up enough; the imbalance between the representation of the two values is too great.

Sensibility in the usage of the time seems commonly to oscillate between two meanings, or to combine both. It can denote a tendency to strong and passionate emotion; or a sensitivity to aesthetic quality and other kinds of refined experience. The question to be asked is whether this novel appears to condemn either thing. Is Jane Austen against strong passion, in love, in other human relations, and in our response to music, art, and literature? And does she feel that too great a value can be put on aesthetic sensitivity, or that aesthetic rapture may be an excessive emotion?

The question about love is the most quickly answered, for it is certainly wrong to suppose that the cultivation of Sense implies a rejection of strong feeling. In a passionate speech Elinor insists to Marianne that she feels and suffers, and that only 'constant and painful exertion' has enabled her to keep the extent of her suffering hidden.[13] Even at the cost of perhaps a little clumsiness, the author seems very keen to make clear to us that Sense does not in the least imply insensibility.

Let us take a look at Colonel Brandon. He, after all, has the most romantic life of any character in any of the novels. He has served as a soldier in the East Indies; he planned to elope with the girl he loved, and was only foiled by the treachery of a dastardly servant; he has rescued a fallen and dying woman from a debtors' prison and undertaken the care of her orphaned child; he fights a duel with Willoughby; he is believed to have fathered a natural daughter but is too proud to confute the rumour; he is sombre and melancholy, evidently nursing a deep and abiding sorrow—yes, the most Byronic figure in Jane Austen's entire canon is Colonel Brandon, the man in the flannel waistcoat.

He is the person to whom the troublesome noun is first applied: once his partiality for Marianne is discovered, he becomes a victim of 'the ridicule so justly annexed to sensibility' (the words are of course heavily ironical: in purporting to disparage sensibility they in effect champion it). And only a page or two later Elinor defends him against the belittlements of Willoughby and Marianne by declaring that he is a man of sense.[14] Of course, sensibility is being used here with a particular significance: it is a polite term for sexual passion. But sexual passion is quite properly classed as a form of sensibility. It is worth stressing that so early in the book there is a person identified as someone in whom both sense and sensibility are combined.

It is also worth observing that at the very end of the book sensibility—in the sense of strong and impulsive feeling, not carefully modulated or moderated—is what, paradoxically, gives Marianne her happiness. 'That Marianne found her own happiness in forming his [Brandon's] was equally the persuasion and delight of each observing friend. Marianne could never love by halves; and her whole heart became in time as much devoted to her husband, as it had once been to Willoughby.'[15] Marianne's warm impulsiveness does not leave her—that is psychologically just—but it also, by a charming irony, fits her for her 'extraordinary fate'. We might reflect that Elinor, the woman of sense, would have been less fitted to make a success of a marriage contracted without love, on a basis of friendship and esteem. Rational esteem, in her case, would have remained just that.

I share the feeling that there is something wrong about the working out of *Sense and Sensibility*, but I suspect that the wrongness is not very great; indeed it may not go much beyond one particular. Jane Austen's misjudgement, if there is one, seems to me to lie not so much in the action of the story as in the conclusion. 'Marianne Dashwood was born to an extraordinary fate. She was born to discover the falsehood of her own opinions, and to counteract, by her conduct, her most favourite maxims.'[16] The demands of epigrammatism and the wish to shape the story to a sharp, decisive ending seem to present an outcome more flat and absolute than the narrative has suggested. Even so, we might note how limited is the reversal in Marianne. Opinions are what she has found false, maxims are what she has counteracted; and sensibility is not primarily a matter of maxims and opinions, but of outlook, style, behaviour, and response. Evidently she has made mistakes, and they are mistakes that a person who places a high value on sensibility may be more likely than others to make: she has been unguarded, overtrustful, self-absorbed, intolerant of those less refined than herself (this last tendency perhaps as much the fault of youth and inexperience as of sensibility). Certainly Jane Austen suggests that sensibility carries dangers with it; but that is not to say that it is necessarily a bad thing in itself. Marianne's emotions are not presented, as they might so easily have been, as assumed or inauthentic; indeed, the book's painfulness lies in the acuteness of her suffering.

Marianne longs 'to have time for atonement to my God'.[17] This is perhaps the most theological utterance in any of the novels; it is wrung out of Marianne's passionate nature, and it is hard to believe that Jane Austen disapproved of it. Both Elinor and Marianne are readers—to the amusement of the philistines around them—but Marianne is the keener reader of the two.[18] This too must be to Jane Austen's liking. We should also notice that she makes both sisters aesthetically creative: Marianne is a musician, and Elinor a graphic artist, who can easily spend a whole day at her drawing board. Contrast Fanny Price, who is deliberately given no interest in learning either to draw or play—or for a more subtle contrast take Emma, who dabbles in reading, drawing, and music without concentrating much attention on any of them. Jane Austen could have contrasted the artistic with the inartistic sister; or more probably, have contrasted the one whose artistic proclivities were exhibited in conspicuous moderation with the one whose aestheticism is conspicuously indulged. But she does neither thing. When *Sense and Sensibility* first came out, some among her acquaintance supposed Jane Austen to have modelled the two heroines upon her sister Cassandra and herself. It was Marianne whom they took for the fictionalized Jane.[19]

The book depicts a struggle between sense and sensibility. But there is also within it a struggle between two ideas: the idea of sense and sensibility being best when they are in equilibrium, and the idea of sense enjoying a triumph over sensibility. And there seems to be a struggle within Jane Austen herself between the assertion of a firm, conclusive moral and a kind of openness. This is a book about a conflict of values or ideas which is at conflict with itself, a book which promises a clarity of conclusion which it fails to deliver. At one moment we may feel the fault to be that the characters are too much types; at another that they are not types enough, and have acquired sufficient autonomy to refuse to fit within the boundaries that the author has designed for them. And we may feel an uncertainty about how far the awkwardness and conflictedness of the book are designed, how far the product of an art not fully mature, a writer not fully in command of her story. Something is not quite right;

and yet the idea that 'something is not quite right' seems to be built into the conclusion as part of its essential character. This imperfect book ends with a picture of imperfection, with Marianne making do. Something somewhere is not quite right; and yet the very imperfection seems to make the book the more searching.

Marianne is thrust into wedlock by the pressure of all those around her:[20]

> With such a confederacy against her—with a knowledge so intimate of his goodness—with a conviction of his fond attachment to herself, which at last, though long after it was observable to everybody else—burst on her—what could she do?

'What could she do?' The use of the question form here is very fine. The narrative shrugs its shoulders, feeling the helplessness of Marianne herself, the combination of causative force and contingency that shapes human lives, the mixture of comedy and something touching at the picture of Marianne's being drawn into marriage with the Colonel. Significantly, Jane Austen uses the question mark again in that other case where the happy marriage is a kind of *pis aller*—when Edmund Bertram, freed of his infatuation for Mary Crawford, begins to think of domestic contentment with Fanny: 'With such a regard for her, indeed, as his had long been, a regard founded on the most endearing claims of innocence and helplessness, and completed by every recommendation of growing worth, what could be more natural than the change?'[21] The narrative looks quizzically upon the odd twists in human affairs, invites us to smile a little, and perhaps feel the touch of poignancy too.

The argument has been put about that Jane Austen preaches female submissiveness in the married state. It is not so. (As an orthodox Christian, she presumably accepted that wives should obey their husbands—whatever that may mean—as required by the Book of Common Prayer; but those who think the books advocate submissiveness mean more than that.) Elizabeth Bennet does not repent of her 'impertinence', but glories in it, and it will, as we are explicitly told, achieve new and more effective forms of expression after her marriage: she will tease and teach her husband as he in other ways will be able to teach her. Elinor Dashwood is made of tougher stuff than her Edward; it is easy to see who will be the stronger partner in that marriage. Anne Elliot takes command after the accident at Lyme, when Wentworth dithers uselessly; their marriage too promises to be a union of independent spirits. Fanny Price's progress, properly understood, includes the achievement of an independence from Edmund which fits her to be his wife. Mary Crawford, who foresees in Fanny an adoringly submissive wife for Henry, not only mistakes her particular character but misjudges the nature of a good marriage as these books portray it. Among the heroines only Catherine Morland threatens to turn into the adoring little woman, significantly in the lightest of the novels—and even Catherine is growing up. Emma, marrying a father-figure, is a special case; but if you are invited to dine at Donwell Abbey, it is Mrs Knightley whom you will expect to provide the sparkle. Among the minor characters, Mrs Palmer's constant praise of her husband makes her a figure of fun, while Mrs Croft is held up to admiration. Her robust and independent spirit takes the form of an adventurous attachment to her husband; this is

Jane Austen's most whole-hearted picture of married love enduring with full success in an older couple. Her ideal seems to be one of complementarity: either the complementarity of similarity, as with Fanny and Edmund or the Crofts; or the complementarity of difference, as with Elizabeth and Darcy, or Marianne and her colonel. None of the heroines is said to find her happiness in a fecund maternity. There is no reason to think that Jane Austen set a low value on motherhood, but the absence of the maternal theme does enable her to present an idea of good marriage simply in terms of the relationship between man and woman (as with the childless Crofts). It is an idea of full partnership, not of submission to a figure of authority.

She was a devout Christian; we know that from her life and from some of her private writings. From her books we can see her belief in the possibility of virtue and happiness. Critics have often been surprised that there is next to no depiction of religious experience in her work, indeed hardly any distinctively religious language, even from Fanny and Edmund. I think that this may have been due to the kind of fastidiousness that led her to keep the nobility out of her novels—a reluctance to indulge her readers, or make too glib appeals to their favour. Sanctimony was as much to be avoided as snob-appeal: had her characters paraded their piety, or been seen taking comfort from prayer, that would have been too easy a play for the readers' approval—or so I suspect Jane Austen may have thought. Though Marianne Dashwood speaks of making atonement to her God, this is significantly in one of the earlier novels; it is a note that Jane Austen will not repeat.

She is keenly conscious of human sinfulness, even when

most brightly comic: none of the novels shows more strongly the malignancy of gossip and competition in Pleasantville than *Pride and Prejudice*. This consciousness is not very well described as 'regulated hatred'. It is perfectly possible to look upon the darkness in human nature with a light spirit (some of the greatest saints have done so). Consider, to take just one example, the bystanders collecting on the Cobb after Louisa Musgrove's accident, 'to be useful if wanted, at any rate, to enjoy the sight of a dead young lady, nay, two dead young ladies, for it proved twice as fine as the first report'.[22] In a sense this gives a black picture of humanity, but one would need a severe deficiency in sense of humour not to see that the author is smiling and not to smile oneself. Conceivably she was a 'Christian pessimist' in that she may have supposed the present state of society to be the best that could be hoped for; it does not seem to me that the evidence, whether within the novels or outside them, is enough either to confirm or confute that possibility.

What must be said emphatically is that she does not praise the existing state of society. As I have argued, even in *Emma*, where the principal landowner is a pattern of paternal virtue, the spiritual leadership of the community is corrupted, Miss Bates is threatened with genteel destitution, experience is narrow and constricted, and the heroine is at risk of being stifled by her father's power over her. Jane Austen likes to see social mobility. Sir Walter Elliot objects to the navy 'as being the means of bringing persons of obscure birth into undue distinction, and raising men to honours which their father and grandfathers never dreamt of',[23] but it would be obvious that the author despises this outlook, even if we had not known about her two sailor brothers (we indeed know, as she never would, that one of them ended as Admiral of the Fleet and a Knight Grand Cross). Several of the most sympathetic characters in the novels are 'trade' or have newly risen from it: Bingley, the Gardiners, Mrs Jennings, the Westons, and Frank Churchill. The people who despise trade are held up to our derision—that is too obvious to need illustration. The comic parvenu or *bourgeois gentilhomme* was a favourite character in books and on the stage for centuries—Mr Dubster in *Camilla* is an example from Jane Austen's own time—but Sir William Lucas is the only example in her own novels, and an understated example at that.

She was a romantic, in the everyday sense that she believed one should marry for love. That is at least implicit everywhere in her work, and it is entirely explicit in *Persuasion*, despite its being perhaps the most chastened and sober in colour of all the novels: Lady Russell was flatly wrong to prevent Anne's marriage to Wentworth and to set the persuasions of prudence above the hunger of the heart. Anne had been 'forced into prudence' and then 'learned romance', 'the natural sequel of an unnatural beginning'.[24] 'Learn' is the crucial word: in Jane Austen's view, romance is a truth about human nature. Four of the heroines turn down proposals of marriage, and except in Emma's case, these would all have been 'good matches'. As things turn out, all these heroines do about as well or better in worldly terms with their eventual husbands (except perhaps for Fanny, who exchanges a substantial landowner for a younger son), but at the time Fanny risks poverty by her refusal and Anne risks being left on the shelf. But for Jane Austen it is better to burn than to marry without love, and her own life bears witness to this conviction.

She is a romantic in that she depicts the game of life as being rightly played for high stakes (in this she is in agreement with Marianne Dashwood and Mary Crawford). Men and women may hope to be deeply happy, but if a gentlewoman should miss the chance of marriage, or take the wrong husband, her existence may be joyless. For most of her book, Fanny Price has the bleakest life of the heroines, but she will finally escape from the emotional desert in which Mrs Norris has wandered all her life. She will not, like Mrs Norris, remain the poor relation for ever, dependent and looked down upon, and she will find a husband whom she loves. Reality could be unkinder. Jane Austen's sister Cassandra lost her fiancé, who died of a fever in the West Indies; she had staked her whole happiness on him, and seems never to have considered another man. Jane herself was soon parted from the first, perhaps the chief love of her life, the young Irishman Tom Lefroy, and never saw him again. Years later, she accepted a proposal from a prosperous, commonplace Hampshire squire, only to withdraw her acceptance the next day. The marriage would have given her money and comfort, but no doubt she said to herself what Mr Bennet said to his Lizzy: 'I know that you could be neither happy nor respectable unless you truly esteemed your husband; unless you looked up to him as a superior. Your lively talents would place you in the greatest danger in an unequal marriage.'[25]

But disappointments in life are best met (these novels imply) with a kind of stoical common sense: we jog along, we make do. Jane Austen represents passion, and even ecstasy, with pleasure and approbation, but if it is romantic to feed and foster the extremes of emotion, to advertise misery and indulge despair, then she is in this respect no romantic. When Mary Crawford talks cynically about marriage, her half-sister Mrs Grant replies:[26]

> My dear child, there must be a little imagination here. I beg your pardon, but I cannot quite believe you. Depend upon it, you see but half. You see the evil, but you do not see the consolation. There will be little rubs and disappointments everywhere, and we are all apt to expect too much; but then, if one scheme of happiness fails, human nature turns to another; if the first calculation is wrong, we make a second better; we find comfort somewhere—...

'We find comfort somewhere.' Mrs Grant is one of those minor characters whom Jane Austen suddenly brings to intense life. We recall that she is a sensible woman, about 30, childless, and married to a husband fifteen years her senior who cares for nothing much except food.[27] After Jane Austen, many novels will dwell upon the misery of unsuccessful marriage, but her own art is more indirect: we have to be very attentive to catch in Mrs Grant's seemingly simple reflections the presence of something like heroism. She speaks lightly, and makes no complaint, but she is evidently drawing on her own experience. Jane Austen too knew enough in her own life of limits, restrictions, disappointed hopes. Such are the realities which lie behind her novels, not concealed or evaded in them, but shaped to the purposes of comedy, with gaiety and courage of heart.

Notes

The novels are cited thus:

MP   *Mansfield Park*
NA   *Northanger Abbey*
Pers.   *Persuasion*
PP   *Pride and Prejudice*
SS   *Sense and Sensibility*

These abbreviations are also used:

Butler   Marilyn Butler, *Jane Austen and the War of Ideas* (Oxford, 1975)
Harding   D. W. Harding, *Regulated Hatred and Other Essays on Jane Austen* (London, 1998)
Memoir   J. E. Austen-Leigh, *A Memoir of Jane Austen*, ed. Kathryn Sutherland, with other family recollections (Oxford (Oxford World's Classics), 2002). The page numbers of the first edition (London, 1870) are given in brackets.
Watt   Ian Watt (ed.), *Jane Austen: A Collection of Critical Essays* (Englewood Cliffs, NJ, 1963)

Chapter 1

1. Curiously, two books with an identical title, *Jane Austen and the Theatre*, appeared in 2002—by Paula Byrne (London) and Penny Gay (Cambridge). As it happens, neither book is interested in the kind of theatrical method of narration that I am concerned with here.
2. *PP* vol. iii, ch. 16.
3. *PP* vol. iii, ch. 17.

4. *PP* vol. iii, ch. 6.
5. *NA* vol. ii, ch. 16.
6. *NA* vol. i, ch. 4.
7. *Emma* vol. iii, ch. 13.
8. Cf. Mary Lascelles, *Jane Austen and her Art* (Oxford, 1939), 162.
9. *PP* vol. iii, ch. 16.
10. *PP* vol. iii, ch. 18.
11. *PP* vol. iii, ch. 18.
12. *PP* vol. iii, ch. 15.
13. *PP* vol. i, ch. 6.
14. *PP* vol. iii, ch. 3.

Chapter 2

1. Letter of 9 Sept. 1814.
2. Claire Tomalin, *Jane Austen* (New York, 1997), ch. 8.
3. Ibid., ch. 15 (p 164).
4. *MP* vol. iii, ch. 17.
5. *NA* first sentence.
6. *NA* vol. ii, ch. 3.
7. *NA* vol. i, ch. 12.
8. *PP* vol. iii, chs. 5 and 8.
9. *PP* vol. iii, ch. 8.
10. *Emma* vol. iii, ch. 11.
11. Harding, ch. 1.
12. *Emma* vol. ii, ch. 8.
13. Among the recent adaptations the BBC's *Persuasion* has been the only one to get the social levels right (the Musgroves at Uppercross, Sir Walter in Bath).
14. Butler, 215.
15. Letter of 4 Feb. 1813.
16. *PP* vol. iii, ch. 14.

Chapter 3

1. *PP* vol. i, ch. 9.
2. *Oliver Twist*, ch. 4. John Carey, *The Violent Effigy* (London, 1973), 68, draws attention to this passage.
3. *MP* vol. iii, ch. 16.

4. *MP* vol. iii, ch. 15.
5. *Emma* vol. i, chs. 13 and 8.
6. *Emma* vol. i, ch. 8; vol. iii, ch. 18.
7. *Emma* vol. i, ch. 11.
8. *Emma* vol. i, ch. 18.
9. *Emma* vol. ii, ch. 2.
10. *Emma* vol. i, ch. 9.
11. *Emma* vol. i, ch. 10.
12. *MP* vol. iii, ch. 2.
13. *MP* vol. i, ch. 3.
14. *PP* vol. iii, ch. 17.
15. *MP* vol. iii, ch. 16.
16. *Emma* vol. ii, ch. 15; vol. iii, ch. 2.
17. *Emma* vol. iii, ch. 17.
18. Harding, ch. 5.
19. *PP* vol. i, ch. 13.
20. *PP* vol. i, chs. 13 and 15.
21. *Meet Mr Mulliner*, 'The Truth about George'.
22. *PP* vol. i, ch. 19.
23. *PP* vol. ii, ch. 8.
24. *PP* vol. i, ch. 5.
25. *Emma* vol. ii, ch. 5.
26. *Emma* vol. i, ch. 13.
27. *Emma* vol. i, ch. 12.
28. *Emma* vol. i, chs. 1 and 11.
29. *Emma* vol. iii, ch. 18.
30. *PP* vol. iii, ch. 15; vol. ii, ch. 18.
31. *PP* vol. ii, chs. 13 and 12; vol. iii, ch. 16.
32. *PP* vol. iii, ch. 16; vol. i, ch. 8.
33. *PP* vol. iii, ch. 18; vol. i, ch. 2; vol. i, ch. 18.
34. *PP* vol. iii, ch. 17.
35. *PP* vol. i, ch. 18.
36. *PP* vol. iii, ch. 10.
37. *PP* vol. i, ch. 2.
38. *PP* vol. iii, ch. 15.
39. *PP* vol. iii, ch. 6.
40. *PP* vol. i, ch. 23.
41. *PP* vol. iii, ch. 15.
42. Letter of 24 May 1813.

43. Crispin, *The Moving Toyshop*, ch. 4. The murderer in this story would have escaped detection, had he not been such a keen Janeite.
44. *PP* vol. i, ch. 10.
45. *PP* vol. i, ch. 16.
46. *PP* vol. i, ch. 18.
47. *PP* vol. ii, ch. 9.
48. *PP* vol. iii, ch. 1.
49. *PP* vol. iii, ch. 10.
50. *PP* vol. ii, ch. 11.
51. *PP* vol. iii, ch. 16.
52. *PP* vol. iii, ch. 16.
53. *PP* vol. iii, ch. 18.
54. *PP* vol. iii, ch. 16.

Chapter 4

1. Amis, 'What Became of Jane Austen?', originally in *Spectator*, 4 Oct. 1957, reprinted in Watt, 141–4, and in *What Became of Jane Austen? And Other Questions* (London, 1970).
2. *MP* vol. iii, ch. 8.
3. *MP* vol. i, ch. 1.
4. *MP* vol. ii, ch. 2.
5. *MP* vol. i, ch. 15.
6. Christopher Ricks notes the 'unforgettable' child's voice here ('Jane Austen and the Business of Mothering', in *Essays in Appreciation* (Oxford, 1996), 90–103, at 98 f).
7. *MP* vol. iii, ch. 1.
8. *MP* vol. i, ch. 3.
9. *NA* vol. ii, ch. 13.
10. *MP* vol. i, ch. 11.
11. *MP* vol. iii, ch. 5.
12. *MP* vol. iii, ch. 3.
13. *MP* vol. i, ch. 2; vol. ii, ch. 7.
14. *MP* vol. iii, ch. 17.
15. *MP* vol. iii, ch. 15.
16. *MP* vol. iii, ch. 17.
17. *MP* vol. iii, ch. 17.
18. *NA* vol. ii, ch. 16.
19. *Memoir*, 119 (140).

20. Lewis, 'A Note on Jane Austen', in Watt, 25–34, at 31 (first in *Essays in Criticism* 4 (1954), 359–71).
21. *The Newcomes*, ch. 31.
22. *Adam Bede*, ch. 17.
23. *MP* vol. i, ch. 4.
24. *MP* vol. i, ch. 12; vol. ii, ch. 3.
25. *MP* vol. i, ch. 2.
26. *MP* vol. iii, ch. 16.
27. *MP* vol. ii, ch. 6.
28. *MP* vol. ii, ch. 11.
29. *MP* vol. i, ch. 3.
30. Letter of 23 Mar. 1817.
31. *MP* vol. i, chs. 12 and 14; vol. ii, ch. 4.
32. *MP* vol. ii, ch. 10.
33. *MP* vol. ii, ch. 10.
34. *MP* vol. iii, ch. 2.
35. *MP* vol. ii, ch. 6.
36. *MP* vol. iii, ch. 10.
37. *MP* vol. iii, ch. 1.
38. *MP* vol. iii, ch. 15.
39. Trilling, *The Opposing Self* (uniform edition, Oxford, 1980), 199 (= Watt, 137).
40. *MP* vol. iii, ch. 6.
41. *MP* vol. i, ch. 16.
42. *MP* vol. ii, ch. 3.
43. *MP* vol. iii, ch. 3.
44. *MP* vol. i, ch. 8.
45. *MP* vol. ii, ch. 4.
46. *MP* vol. i, ch. 11.
47. *MP* vol. i, ch. 7.
48. *MP* vol. i, ch. 6.
49. *MP* vol. i, ch. 6. This is a puzzle. Intuitively one feels that so coarse a joke cannot be intended by a polite lady novelist of Regency date. But a pun on 'Vices' alone seems too weak for Miss Crawford, and the italicizations indicate that 'Rears' too is part of the innuendo.
50. *MP* vol. i, ch. 15.
51. *MP* vol. ii, ch. 1.
52. *MP* vol. i, ch. 13.
53. *MP* vol. i, ch. 14.

54. *MP* vol. iii, ch. 4.
55. *MP* vol. iii, ch. 13.
56. *MP* vol. i, ch. 1.
57. John Sutherland, *Is Heathcliff a Murderer?* (Oxford, 1996), 1 and 9, suggests that Tom, broken in health, is unlikely to father an heir, so that we must expect Fanny ultimately to inhabit Mansfield Park as Lady Bertram. This is very naughty.
58. *MP* vol. iii, ch. 17.
59. *PP* vol. iii, ch. 16.
60. *MP* vol. iii, ch. 16.
61. *MP* vol. iii, ch. 16.
62. *MP* vol. iii, ch. 17.
63. *MP* vol. ii, ch. 12.
64. *MP* vol. ii, ch. 12.
65. *NA* vol. ii, ch. 15.
66. *MP* vol. iii, ch. 17.
67. *MP* vol. i, chs. 5 and 14.
68. *MP* vol. iii, ch. 10.
69. *MP* vol. iii, ch. 10.
70. *MP* vol. iii, ch. 11.
71. *MP* vol. iii, ch. 3.
72. *MP* vol. iii, ch. 12.
73. *MP* vol. ii, ch. 12.
74. *MP* vol. i, ch. 7; vol. ii, ch. 7.
75. *MP* vol. iii, ch. 2.
76. *MP* vol. iii, ch. 5.
77. *MP* vol. ii, ch. 6.
78. *MP* vol. ii, ch. 12.
79. *MP* vol. iii, ch. 5.
80. *MP* vol. iii, ch. 11.
81. *MP* vol. iii, ch. 9.
82. *MP* vol. i, ch. 8; vol. ii, ch. 5.
83. *MP* vol. ii, ch. 7.
84. *MP* vol. i, ch. 2.
85. *MP* vol. i, ch. 4.
86. *MP* vol. ii, ch. 3.
87. *MP* vol. i, ch. 9.
88. *MP* vol. i, ch. 10.
89. *MP* vol. iii, chs. 7 and 9; *Emma* vol. iii, ch. 4.

90. *MP* vol. i, ch. 1; vol. iii, ch. 1.
91. *MP* vol. iii, ch. 1.
92. *MP* vol. iii, ch. 5.

Chapter 5

1. *PP* vol. i, ch. 7.
2. *PP* vol. iii, ch. 11.
3. *Emma* vol. i, ch. 16.
4. *Memoir*, 71 (109).
5. Caroline Austen, in the Oxford World's Classics edition of the *Memoir*, 173.
6. *Emma* vol. i, ch. 1.
7. *Emma* vol. ii, ch. 18.
8. *Emma* vol. iii, ch. 6.
9. *Emma* vol. i, ch. 11.
10. *Emma* vol. i, chs. 17 and 18; vol. ii, ch. 14.
11. *Emma* vol. ii, ch. 18.
12. *Emma* vol. i, ch. 5.
13. *Emma* vol. i, ch. 3.
14. *Emma* vol. i, chs. 5 and 18; vol. ii, ch. 2.
15. *Emma* vol. i, ch. 1; vol. ii, ch. 6.
16. *Emma* vol. iii, ch. 12.
17. *Emma* vol. ii, ch. 8.
18. *Emma* vol. ii, chs. 12 and 13.
19. *PP* vol. i, ch. 15; *SS* vol. i, ch. 7.
20. *Emma* vol. i, chs. 1 and 3.
21. *Emma* vol. i, ch. 1.
22. *Emma* vol.i, ch. 2.
23. *Emma* vol. ii, ch. 3; vol. i, ch. 1.
24. *Emma* vol. i, ch. 17.
25. *Emma* vol. ii, ch. 5.
26. *Emma* vol. ii, ch. 14.
27. *Emma* vol. i, ch. 1.
28. *Emma* vol. i, ch. 9.
29. *Emma* vol. i, ch. 5.
30. *Pers.* vol. i, ch. 1.
31. *Emma* vol. i, ch. 13.
32. *Emma*, e.g. vol. ii, ch. 8.

33. *Emma* vol. iii, ch. 2.
34. *Emma* vol. ii, ch. 9.
35. *Emma* vol. i, chs. 1 and 2.
36. *Emma* vol. i, chs. 11 and 15.
37. *Emma* vol. i, ch. 11.
38. *Emma* vol. iii, ch. 17.
39. *Emma* vol. ii, ch. 13; vol. iii, ch. 17.
40. *Emma* vol. i, ch. 3.
41. *Emma* vol. i, ch. 13.
42. *Emma* vol. ii, ch. 7.
43. *Emma* vol. iii, ch. 6.
44. *Emma* vol. i, ch. 10.
45. *Memoir*, 119 (140).
46. David Nokes, *Jane Austen* (New York, 1997), 459.
47. Marvin Mudrick, *Jane Austen: Irony as Defense and Discovery* (Princeton, 1952), 185.
48. *Emma* vol.ii, chs. 6 and 7.
49. *Emma* vol. i, ch. 10.
50. *Emma* vol. iii, ch. 6.
51. Jane Austen had a pattern for this theme in Fanny Burney's *Cecilia*, in which the heroine takes up the sweet, pretty, simple, adoring Henrietta (a name very similar to Harriet), and finds, like Emma, that her protégée is in love with the same man as herself. Burney presents this patronage as one more example of Cecilia's wondrous virtue; Jane Austen of course sees more moral complexity, but the impulse is benevolent.
52. *Emma* vol. i, ch. 5.
53. *Emma* vol. i, chs. 1 and 4.
54. *Emma* vol. iii, ch. 13.
55. *Emma* vol. iii, ch. 15.
56. *Emma* vol. iii, ch. 13.
57. *Emma* vol. iii, ch. 18.
58. *Emma* vol. iii, ch. 14.
59. *Emma* vol. iii, ch. 18.
60. *Emma* vol. iii, ch. 14.

Chapter 6

1. *Pers.* vol. ii, ch. 12.
2. *Pers.* vol. i, ch. 6.

3. *Memoir*, 118 (202).
4. Letter of 11 Dec. 1815.
5. 'Eleusinian mysteries': George Eliot, *Scenes of Clerical Life*, 'Amos Barton', ch. 2.
6. *MP* vol. iii, ch. 7.
7. *Emma* vol. ii, ch. 6; *PP* vol. i, ch. 8.
8. *NA* vol. i, ch. 14.
9. *MP* vol. iii, ch. 13.
10. Butler, 96 ff., 108 ff.
11. *Memoir*, 116 (197).
12. *SS* vol. i, ch. 16.
13. *SS* vol. iii, ch. 1.
14. *SS* vol. i, ch. 10.
15. *SS* vol. iii, ch. 14.
16. *SS* vol. iii, ch. 14.
17. *SS* vol. iii, ch. 10.
18. *SS* vol. iii, ch. 6.
19. *Memoir*, 19 (27).
20. *SS* vol. iii, ch. 14.
21. *MP* vol. iii, ch. 17.
22. *Pers.* vol. i, ch. 12.
23. *Pers.* vol. i, ch. 3.
24. *Pers.* vol. i, ch. 4.
25. *PP* vol. iii, ch. 17.
26. *MP* vol. i, ch. 5.
27. *MP* vol. i, ch. 3.

Sources and Further Reading

The standard edition of the novels is that of R. W. Chapman (3rd edn., London, 1993). A further volume, containing the juvenilia and unfinished works, was added in 1954, and has been frequently reprinted with revisions. (The Oxford World's Classics series now makes the juvenilia available as *Catharine and Other Writings* and the unfinished works of her maturity in a volume including *Northanger Abbey*.) A new scholarly edition with commentary is in preparation, to be published by Cambridge University Press.

Our knowledge of Jane Austen's life derives mostly from two sources, her letters and the reminiscences of her family, principally the children and other descendants of her eldest brother James. The letters are edited by Deirdre Le Faye (*Jane Austen's Letters* (Oxford, 1995), a revision of earlier editions by R. W. Chapman). *A Memoir of Jane Austen*, by James Edward Austen-Leigh (James Austen's son) remains fundamental (London, 1870 (2nd edn., 1871). It is now most easily found in the Oxford World's Classics series (2002), edited with introduction and notes by Kathryn Sutherland; this volume also includes the shorter memoirs by Henry Austen, Jane's brother, and Anna Lefroy and Caroline Austen (James Austen's two daughters). There is important material too in *Jane Austen: A Family Record* (London, 1989), a revision and enlargement by Deirdre Le Faye of a *Life and Letters of Jane Austen* by William Austen-Leigh and R. A. Austen-Leigh, published in 1913, and about Jane's family in *Austen Papers 1704–1856*, edited by R. A. Austen-Leigh (privately printed [London], 1942).

From among recent lives I have drawn principally on Claire Tomalin, *Jane Austen* (New York, 1997). There are several other biographies. David Nokes, *Jane Austen* (New York, 1997), is best avoided. George Holbert Tucker, *A History of Jane Austen's Family* (rev. edn., Stroud, 1998), is exactly what its title says (first published in 1983 as *A Goodly Heritage*).

Among older books on the novels, two that still draw readers are Mary

SOURCES AND FURTHER READING

Lascelles, *Jane Austen and her Art* (Oxford, 1939), and Marvin Mudrick, *Jane Austen: Irony as Defense and Discovery* (Princeton, 1952). D. W. Harding, 'Regulated Hatred: An Aspect of the Work of Jane Austen', *Scrutiny*, 8 (1940), 346–62, is probably the most influential single article written about her. I cite it and another of his pieces, 'Character and Caricature in Jane Austen' (first in B. C. Southam (ed.), *Critical Essays on Jane Austen* (London, 1968)), from *Regulated Hatred and Other Essays on Jane Austen* (London, 1998). Ian Watt (ed.), *Jane Austen: A Collection of Critical Essays* (Englewood Cliffs, NJ, 1963), reprints some notable articles and extracts from books, including Harding's 'Regulated Hatred . . .', Lionel Trilling, '*Mansfield Park*' (from *The Opposing Self* (uniform edn., Oxford, 1980)), C. S. Lewis, 'A Note on Jane Austen' (originally in *Essays in Criticism*, 4 (1954), 359–71), and Kingsley Amis's short assault on *Mansfield Park*, 'What Became of Jane Austen?'

Marilyn Butler's important and influential work *Jane Austen and the War of Ideas* (Oxford, 1975; reissued with a new introduction, 1987) pioneered the study of the novelist in relation to the social and cultural politics of the time. She is richly informative on other novelists active in the period. It will be evident to readers of her book and mine, however, that I doubt her central argument. Mary Evans, *Jane Austen and the State* (London, 1987), talks sense about its subject. The sexual politics of the novels have been much discussed, for example by Margaret Kirkham, *Jane Austen, Feminism, and Fiction* (Brighton, 1983) and Claudia Johnson, *Jane Austen: Women, Politics, and the Novel* (Chicago, 1988). Edward Said's discussion of *Mansfield Park* in his *Culture and Imperialism* (London, 1993), 100–16, inaugurated a vogue for post-colonial and other self-consciously 'transgressive' readings of Jane Austen. Vulnerable though Said's analysis is, both factually and as interpretation, this might at least be said: it is more remarkable that Jane Austen should mention the slave trade at all than that she should say so little about it.

The Cambridge Companion to Jane Austen, edited by Edward Copeland and Juliet McMaster (Cambridge, 1997), includes besides much else of value a chapter by Bruce Stovel on 'Further Reading' giving guidance through the modern bibliography (see too Claudia Johnson on 'Austen Cults and Cultures'). Books published since include Clara Tuite, *Romantic Austen: Sexual Politics and the Literary Canon* (Cambridge, 2002) and Bharat Tandon, *Jane Austen and the Morality of Conversation* (2003).

To an unusual degree Jane Austen has attracted amateurs to write about her—that is to say, those who are not professional experts on the English novel or the period around 1800—and some of the most telling examinations of her have come from such outsiders or from an oblique approach (D. W.

Harding, by the way, was a psychologist by trade). Particularly interesting are an essay by the eminent philosopher Gilbert Ryle, 'Jane Austen and the Moralists' (*Collected Papers* (London, 1971), i. 276–91), the historian Oliver MacDonagh's *Jane Austen: Real and Imagined Worlds* (New Haven, 1991), which among other virtues understands the nature of religion in her life and novels, and Christopher Ricks, 'Jane Austen and the Business of Mothering', in his *Essays in Appreciation* (Oxford, 1996), 90–103, which attacks from an unusual angle and penetrates deep.

Index

INDEX

215